WASATCH TOURS

A Ski Touring Guide
to the Wasatch Front

by

ALEXIS KELNER
DAVID HANSCOM

Salt Lake City, Utah

For Eric and Brett and Greg.

Bill Rosqvist, Sponsoring Editor

Library of Congress Catalog Card Number 76-28112

ISBN 0-915272-06-7

CONTENTS

8 AMERICAN FORK CANYON

PREFACE

The task of assembling a ski touring guide for the Wasatch Mountains was undertaken after several years of contemplating the magnitude of the task. It seemed obvious that such a guide was needed. Every year a great deal of touring equipment is sold to Utahns who are starting out in the sport. These people need to know where to find suitable terrain for their interests. Also, many people have discovered the hard way that there is more to touring in the Wasatch than climbing up a canyon and sliding back down. The hazards of avalanches and changing weather are very real. Tourers should always be aware of the potential dangers, and they should know how to avoid situations that could end in tragedy.

We would like to acknowledge the assistance of the people who contributed to the project. First and foremost is Larry Swanson, without whose time and flying skills the aerial photographs would not have been possible. His expertise with an airplane made the use of telephoto lenses unnecessary.

Several people studied the avalanche chapter, including Ron Perla, director of avalanche research for the Canadian government, Gerry Horton, Cliff Blake and Jim Head of the Wasatch National Forest, Knox Williams and Pete Martinelli of the U.S. Forest Service Snow and Avalanche Research Project in Fort Collins, Colorado. Their comments were greatly appreciated. We feel that this is the most important part of the book for anyone who tours in the Wasatch Mountains, and their expertise helped to make it accurate.

7

Many friends have assisted in the task of putting this book together. Roly Pearson spent a great deal of his time helping us make photographs and illustrations. Bill Rosqvist and Mel Davis of Wasatch Publishers proofread the text and laid up the type. Numerous others have read parts of the rough draft and made valuable suggestions on its content. Our families have provided "patience and understanding," without which this book would not have been possible. We thank them all very much.

One final comment is in order. We have made an effort in this book to emphasize the avalanche hazards associated with touring in the Wasatch. The most obvious slide paths are marked on the photos, but these are by no means all of the areas where they occur. Any skier who ventures into the Wasatch Mountains must be constantly alert to this prevailing danger. □

Alexis Kelner
Dave Hanscom

MAPS

Photo courtesy of Mel Davis.

1 INTRODUCTION

The Wasatch Mountains east of Salt Lake have long been a favorite haunt of avid downhill skiers from all over the world. An abundance of powder snow, good terrain for any skiing ability, and clear sunny days have made Utah one of the most popular winter recreation areas in the country. There are now six ski areas within 45 minutes of downtown Salt Lake City, and others are in the talking stages. The "white gold" that covers the Wasatch has created a boom in the winter tourist business that significantly helps Utah's economy.

While the ski lifts and condominiums have been multiplying, another boom has been taking place in the mountains. Ski touring has matured from the sport enjoyed by a few hardy mountaineers and racers, to a pastime for almost anyone who has the desire and ambition to take a walk on a winter day. With increasing numbers of people looking for types of recreation that provide fresh air and exercise, this is a natural in the season when tennis, golf, bicycling and hiking aren't possible.

There are as many reasons for ski touring as there are participants in the sport. To some, it is just an extension of hiking, with the possible added benefit of not getting sore knees and feet. (It should be noted that beginning tourers sometimes experience discomfort in other parts of their anatomy while going downhill.) Many skiers want to take advantage of the

Figure 1-1—With commercial ski developments and condominiums spreading into more and more canyon areas, and with bigger crowds coming to Utah from all over the world, ski touring is becoming an attractive alternative for those who enjoy winter solitude. (Photo courtesy of Citizens Committee to Save Our Canyons.)

unlimited trackless powder with no lift ticket to buy or crowd to hassle. Others feel the need to ascend the highest peaks, regardless of the adversity to be surmounted. Whatever the motivation for getting out, Wasatch tourers will find useful information in the pages that follow. The goal of this book is to help people enjoy pleasant and safe ski outings in the back country of the mountains near Salt Lake City.

TOURING AREAS IN THE WASATCH FRONT

The area described in this book is shown on the map in Fig. 1-2. Included are the canyons from Millcreek on the north to American Fork on the south, between the Salt Lake valley on the west and the Park City ridge on the east. There are many other places to enjoy a winter outing within an hour or so of downtown Salt Lake City, but the scope of this guide is limited to the closest and most heavily used areas. Excellent opportunities exist for tours in the Uinta Mountains, for example. They are so numerous, in fact, that another book could be written about that area alone. The Snyderville/Park City/Midway region on the east side of the Wasatch Mountains also offers many possibilities. These were not included for two reasons. First, many of the routes are on jeep roads, which are well marked by snowmobiles and thus easy to follow. Second, there is a great deal of private land at the mouths of most of the canyons, and many owners are understandably reluctant to have large numbers of people crossing their property.

Millcreek Canyon, which comes into the valley at 38th South, is the closest touring area to Salt Lake City. It is plowed only to the Wasatch National Forest Guard Station and allows easy access to the snow. The only side canyon which offers good touring and which is directly accessible by car is Porter Fork. Alexander Basin, Wilson Fork, Soldier Fork, Big and Little Water Gulches, and upper Millcreek are most easily approached from Big Cottonwood Canyon. Touring from one canyon to the other unfortunately involves a car shuttle unless you want to take your chances at hitchhiking. Millcreek Canyon is typical of the Wasatch Mountains in that the terrain is generally steeper on the north slope than on the south. Also the ski touring is generally more difficult in the side canyons that are closer to the valley due partly to steeper slopes and partly to the denser brush that grows at lower elevations. The quality of the snow is usually better in the higher areas.

Neff Canyon begins above the Mount Olympus Cove area of Salt Lake County at about 4200 South. It offers a variety of intermediate and advanced terrain to the skier who is willing to take a chance on snow conditions and who is not too faint-hearted to attempt the narrow trail down to the valley. Because the mouth of Neff Canyon has an elevation of only 5600 feet, the snow there is usually marginal, and the scrub oak beside the trail is impenetrable. The upper part of the canyon, however, has some open areas with two large bowls for the powder lover. It is one of the last "undiscovered" touring areas in the Wasatch.

Big Cottonwood Canyon, which begins at 72nd South, offers the greatest variety of readily accessible ski touring areas in the Wasatch. The north slope is too steep to be skiable below Mill A Gulch; in fact, avalanches in some of the gullies in that area often reach the highway. In 1875 several people were killed when a snow slide wiped out the sawmill that used to be near the mouth of Mill A. Between Mill D and Brighton, however, the terrain is quite gentle, with many excellent beginner and intermediate touring areas on both sides of the road. Actually, the

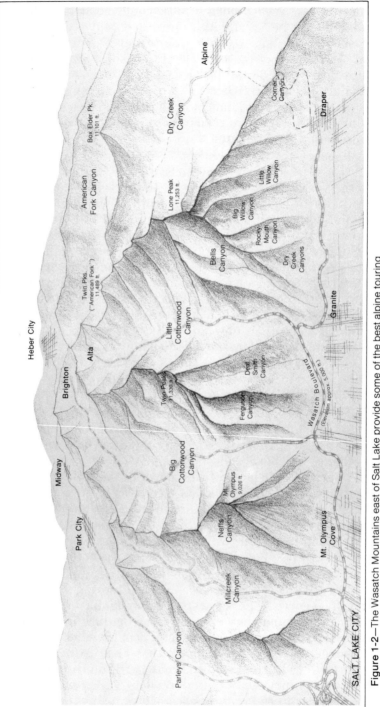

Figure 1-2—The Wasatch Mountains east of Salt Lake provide some of the best alpine touring terrain in the country. Most of the tours described in this book are in one of four major canyons: Millcreek, Big Cottonwood, Little Cottonwood and American Fork.

14

canyon bottom is wide enough in this section to allow a skier to parallel the road for several miles of relatively flat touring. On the south side of Big Cottonwood, the canyons are suitable for touring all the way down to Broads Fork, although Mill B and Broads are quite steep and brushy in the lower sections.

Little Cottonwood Canyon, which starts at about 90th South, is a hub of intermediate and advanced ski touring activity in the Wasatch. It has a good variety of convenient touring terrain starting with Hogum Fork and going all the way to Albion Basin. The north side is extremely steep and rocky and does not lend itself to anything but rock climbing and avalanches. On the south side, however, the forks from Hogum to White Pine have some of the best intermediate and advanced touring in the Wasatch. Gad Valley and Peruvian Gulch were also in that category at one time, but in recent years the snow has developed a serious case of the "mogul disease." We hope this affliction is not allowed to spread into other nearby canyons. Grizzly Gulch and Albion Basin in upper Little Cottonwood have quite gentle terrain for beginning and intermediate tourers. Many other trips that end in Big Cottonwood or American Fork are started in Little Cottonwood to get an elevation advantage.

American Fork Canyon is approached by Utah Route 80 south of "Point of the Mountain". The highway is plowed only to the Tibble Fork Reservoir, so access to the good skiing canyons is best from upper Little Cottonwood. This involves a car shuttle of an hour or more, so these tours are best attempted with the help of a friend to drop you off and pick you up at the other end. All the side canyons in American Fork are extremely steep and hazardous except Mineral Basin, which is of intermediate difficulty. The tours all include some south facing slopes, which often have less-than-ideal snow conditions, but if circumstances are right, this canyon provides some very exciting skiing. The canyon bottom itself is quite flat all the way to the end, but heavy snowmobile traffic generally assures an easy run down to the reservoir.

TOURING EQUIPMENT

One reason for the rapid growth of ski touring is the recent revolution in equipment manufacturing techniques. The sport is no longer restricted to those willing to get messy pine tar up to their elbows or to those strong enough to drag downhill skis and sealskins up a mountain. The wide variety of equipment available today provides many alternatives to the tourer, but it often

Figure 1-3—The thrill of a good run in the powder is surpassed only by the relaxation of a well-planned lunch with your favorite skiing companion.

leads to many hours of confused debate with friends, ski shop employees, and other self-appointed "experts" in such matters. This book does not attempt to answer all the questions that arise on the subject. There are too many new things available each year. We attempt only to help you ask the right questions and give a few examples of the possibilities that exist.

The most important thing to think about is what type of touring you plan to do. Will you stay on relatively flat terrain, or do you like steep powder slopes? Do you usually ski straight down a trail, or do you prefer to wiggle between the trees? Are you satisfied with ski tours in protected areas at lower elevations, or is getting to the top of the ridge or mountain your only reason for going out in the winter? Do you take a ski lift wherever possible and choose trips with a minimum amount of climbing? Are your outings only a few hours long and in good weather, or will you be exposed to severe weather conditions for many hours or days? You will most likely answer yes to several of these questions; therefor equipment buying will involve some compromises.

16

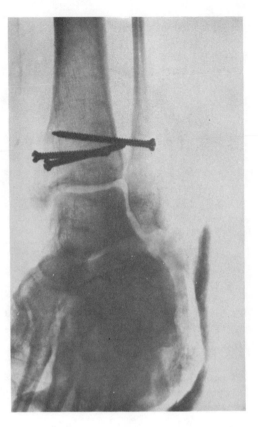

Figure 1-4—Many skiers are understandably reluctant to sacrifice safety for better downhill control. This x-ray is a grim reminder that even a tourer can get "screwed up" if equipment is not chosen carefully.

A second consideration is your skiing ability. Do you have to traverse and kick-turn to survive on any downhill run, or can you make parallel turns with little effort? Do you need light powder in order to ski comfortably, or can you handle more difficult snow conditions? Or maybe you haven't yet been weaned from the packed slopes.

The third area to explore is the inside of your pocketbook. Can you afford expensive new equipment, or will your budget allow only the lowest-cost approach to the sport? Will you have to settle for one set of touring gear for all occasions, or can you buy two types to meet different needs?

Another important factor is the amount of hassle you'll put up with to get the desired performance from your equipment. Are you willing to put a pine tar base on wood skis two or three times a year, or don't you even want to bother to learn about waxing for different snow conditions? Can you stand to

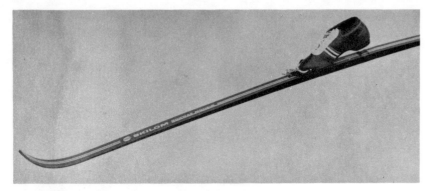

Figure 1-5—Traditional cross country equipment is still the most popular choice the world over. Skis, boots, and bindings are light enough to allow easy climbing, but sturdy enough to survive all but the worst crashes. (Equipment courtesy of Timberline Sports, Inc.)

be miserable once in a while because you can't find the right wax? Do you want to wrestle sealskins on and off wherever your tour route changes from down to up, or vice versa?

Finally, there is the issue of safety. Do you feel the need for release bindings in all of your skiing? Are you willing to incur some risk at times in order to have more downhill control? Do snowshoes sound like the only safe alternative for winter travel in the mountains?

So much for the questions. Four different types of equipment have been chosen to illustrate what alternatives are available. A description of each follows, along with a discussion of its strengths and weaknesses. These are not the only possibilities, but they are all commonly used.

Light Touring Equipment

The lightest-weight touring equipment suitable for general use in the Wasatch Mountains is the "tur-langrenn" or light touring ski with pin bindings and ankle-high boots. A typical setup is shown in Fig. 1-5. The skis are usually 50 to 55 mm wide under the foot and weigh about four pounds. Lighter and narrower skis are available, but they tend to sink farther into deep snow, and they break more easily in a fall. Saving a few ounces is not a good trade-off for mountain touring. Light touring skis are available in traditional wood (the most durable models have Norwegian-type construction with hickory base

18

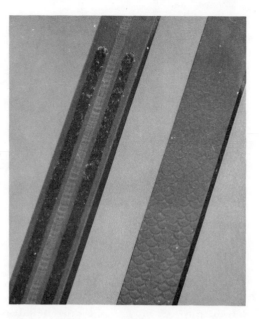

Figure 1-6—Several alternatives exist for tourers who prefer to avoid the waxing dilemma. Most common is a plastic bottom with steps to prevent back-sliding. The other skis shown here have mohair strips embedded in the base. (Equipment courtesy of Timberline Sports, Inc.)

and laminations), and in the new fiberglass materials. The latter are more expensive but much stronger; they also can be stiffer and more difficult to turn in soft snow. Wood models often have edges made of lignostone, which is pressed beech wood, and which wears much longer.

Alternatives for the bottom of the skis include wood, plastic, and waxless types with fishscales or mohair strips. The wood bases are the least expensive option, but they require more care. A sealer (such as pine tar) must be applied at least once a year. Plastic bottoms are more durable and generally faster on the downhill, but wax doesn't adhere to the plastic as well, and great care must be taken when removing old wax. Waxless bases eliminate the need for applying gooey sealers and climbing waxes, but they are much slower on the flats and downhills, and they are more difficult to turn.

Light touring boots have traditionally been made of leather, but synthetic materials are becoming more common. The synthetics are sometimes less expensive, but many people find that they crease uncomfortably at the toe and that they are often cold because they don't breathe well. The soles of light touring boots must be thin enough to fit into pin bindings, so this boot usually doesn't provide a great deal of warmth, and lacks the stiffness necessary for easy turning in deep snow. For powder skiing, the soles with the greatest tortional stiffness (i.e., the

19

Figure 1-7—Some kind of reinforcement in the toe of the boot is important to help withstand the constant twisting that is inevitable in deep snow skiing. (Equipment courtesy of Timberline Sports, Inc.)

ones that are the hardest to *twist)* give the most turning power. This type of boot should be large enough to wear a light and a heavy pair of wool socks and still leave room for plenty of toe movement. It is important that the toes not be tight or they will get pinched whenever a ski slips back while climbing. Light touring boots can be made warmer with insoles or with overboots. A pair of large wool socks over the boot is another possibility, but be sure the bindings function properly with them on.

One final comment concerns the importance of reinforcing the toe of light touring boots so the pin bindings don't tear out. If holes are drilled in the soles, metal plates should be used on the boots. The alternative to drilling holes is to attach a hard rubber piece to the bottom of the boot toe for the pins to go into. An advantage of the latter approach is that the boots fit into bindings with any pin configuration.

Pin bindings have also been revolutionized in recent years. Most manufacturers are making one-piece step-in models in place of (or in addition to) the hand-latching types. Some of the newer models are spring loaded, so the strength of the binding depends upon the strength of the spring mechanism. These can be quite flimsy and have proven to be unreliable for the amount of twisting required for turning (and falling) in deep snow. On the positive side, the newer bindings are being built to a standard 3-pin pattern with a standard boot outline to make it easier to change equipment. Finally, a most important part of the bindings, regardless of model, is some type of heel piece that prevents the boot from sliding sideways on the ski. (Fig. 1-8.)

Light touring equipment is at its best on fairly gentle

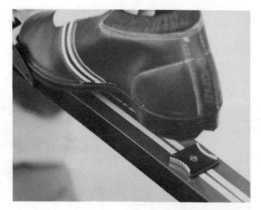

Figure 1-8—Touring bindings are not complete without a heel piece that prevents the boot from sliding off the ski in a turn. Without this simple fixture, even a good powder skier would have difficulty in deep snow. (Equipment courtesy of Timberline Sports, Inc.)

terrain. It is delightful for climbing all but the steepest slopes, but most people have difficulty turning the skis in deep snow. An expert powder skier, however, can usually manage quite steep downhill runs as long as the snow is relatively consistent. The problem is not so much that the skis won't turn, but that the margin for error is very small. Mistakes too often result in a cold landing.

Heavy Touring Equipment

The second category of touring equipment is the heavy touring or mountaineering ski with bindings that can be adjusted to hold the heels down and boots that come above the ankle. These are shown in Fig. 1-9. The skis are usually 55 to 60 mm wide in the center and weigh about six pounds. They are available with or without metal edges. Skis with edges provide much better control on hard snow and are stronger. To be sure, the edges also add weight and cost, but if these were your big worries, you'd be buying light touring skis. Mountaineering skis are available in wood or fiberglass, and with bottoms of the wood, plastic, or waxless types. The trade-offs are the same as for "tur langrenns." The wider skis are suitable for climbing skins, so if particularly steep climbs are to be encountered, a pair of skins would be a good investment.

Heavy touring boots usually come above the ankle and have fairly thick soles. Thus, they provide much more lateral stability for turning and more warmth than the lighter boots discussed previously. They should be large enough for heavy and light wool socks with plenty of toe room, and if extra

Figure 1-9—The ski mountaineer and the aspiring powder skier both need equipment that is sturdy enough to enable them to make turns in challenging terrain and difficult snow conditions. Heavy touring equipment is a good compromise.

warmth is desired, a pair of insoles helps considerably. One way to save money is to use a pair of old downhill boots, preferably of the lace type, that have lost their stiffness. (Try the Salvation Army or Deseret Industries for a starter.) Another possibility is to use hiking boots, but this puts some constraints on choice of bindings.

Cable bindings have traditionally been used with mountaineering skis. Some of them require the square soles of ski boots, but many models are adaptable to hiking boot soles. The disadvantage of cables is that they are generally not a reliable safety binding when the cables are held down at the heel. The friction of the cable in the guides is too great and tends to vary. Some people attach the cables only under the toe except in situations where the skiing is too difficult to handle with the heels free. That may not be a wise trade-off since those are probably the times when safety bindings are most needed.

Several alternatives to cables have become available in recent years. Some of the binding manufacturers are making touring models which can be adjusted to allow heel lift on the uphills, but which convert to a normal release binding for the descent. These are quite heavy and very expensive, but they provide the same degree of safety that one expects in alpine skiing. They also require a square-toed ski boot and a particularly heavy-duty mountaineering ski.

It should be obvious that mountaineering ski equipment

Figure 1-10—Several binding manufacturers now offer convertible models which allow heel-lift for climbing (left), but become normal release types for downhill (right). The safety feature is more important for sturdier skis and boots. (Equipment courtesy of Timberline Sports, Inc.)

is much better for downhill, but less advantageous for climbing, than the light touring option. It provides more stability and allows more margin for error in deep snow skiing. The boots are warmer and thus more suitable for extended tours in very cold weather. Heavy touring gear is good for the learning powder skier who can't resist the steep slopes, and for the person who does a wide variety of tours, but can't afford more than one set of equipment.

Downhill Skiing Equipment

Ski touring in the Wasatch Mountains ten years ago was done almost exclusively on downhill skis, with heavy boots and cable bindings, and with sealskins* strapped to the bottom of the skis to allow uphill progress. This alternative is still the best for tours that have very steep ascents and downhill runs which are of sufficient difficulty to require maximum control. The equipment is very heavy and will make climbing much slower, but there are times when touring equipment just won't suffice. The trend to shorter skis is significantly helping the weight problem; 170 cm. skis are a lot easier to carry than 210's!

Many skiers use touring wax instead of climbers on the

---

*While in the past "sealskins" were actually made from the skin of seals, today's improved climbers are made from synthetic materials, such as mohair.

Figure 1-11—Until recently most ski touring in the Wasatch was done on downhill skis with climbing skins strapped on the bottom. The equipment is quite heavy for ascending, but it provides good control for steep descents and variable snow.

bottom of their alpine skis. It must be applied in a heavier layer and more frequently than on wooden bottoms, and it is not sufficient for steep slopes. Skins need only be used on slopes where traversing back and forth is undesirable. The new bindings which can be adjusted to allow heel lift for climbing, and which convert to release bindings, are certainly the best alternative for downhill skis. (Fig. 1-10.)

The cost of skis, boots, bindings, and climbers is much higher for this alternative than for regular touring equipment. If you do any lift skiing, however, the same set of gear could be used for both, so this approach could actually be the least expensive in the long run.

Snowshoes

Last but not least are the snowshoes. They provide a good firm foundation both going up and coming down, with no slipping and sliding except on really steep terrain. Snowshoes are suitable for most beginner and intermediate tours. Anyone who worries a lot about going too fast on skis and taking a dangerous spill will be much more comfortable on snowshoes. It certainly sounds dull to a confirmed skier, but the snowshoers get the last laugh on very narrow trails where there isn't room enough to make turns to slow down on skis. If hiking is your bag but skiing is not, snowshoes are a good way to get into the mountains in the winter.

Figure 1-12—Snowshoes are a good choice for anyone desiring maximum stability on snow with little risk of losing control and taking a spill. They are also used for carrying very heavy loads over all but the steepest terrain.

Snowshoes are available in wood, metal, or plastic, with laces made of rawhide or neoprene-coated nylon. Aluminum frames are more expensive than wood, but are lighter and require less maintenance. Neoprene resists water absorption and is easier to care for than rawhide. Most plastic showshoes are not a good buy for someone seriously undertaking the sport.

The most important consideration when buying snowshoeing equipment is the quality of the bindings. They must hold the boots firmly, but allow enough freedom for comfortable walking. They must be strong enough to allow pulling and twisting without breaking. Poor quality bindings will lead to no end of problems.

One feature that can be very helpful on hard snow is the snowshoe crampon. This is a device which is attached to the bottom of the frame or binding to provide additional traction. It usually has several sharp teeth which bite into the snow and prevent the shoes from sliding. This would be a valuable item for tours that involve steep slopes or windblown ridges.

Figure 1-13—Ski poles should be long enough to provide support and help forward progress in deep snow. Note the strips of tape around the tonkin poles to provide extra strength, and the large baskets for deep snow.

Snowshoeing is probably the least expensive form of winter touring, especially for someone who already owns hiking boots. Other than the snowshoes, the only other equipment needed is a pair of ski poles.

General Comments

So much for touring equipment alternatives. This section will be concluded with a few general remarks that are applicable to any type of equipment.

- Try to rent or borrow before buying to be sure that ski touring is really for you, and if so, that your choice of equipment was right.
- Ski length should be six to ten inches longer than you are tall, depending on your weight. Extremely short skis tend

to sink too far into deep snow, and longer ones are more difficult to maneuver. The exception is for downhill skis, which are heavier and more difficult to carry. The greater width of these skis provides sufficient flotation to make shorter lengths feasible.

- Pole length should be greater than for downhill skiing to allow more pushing power. A good rule of thumb is arm-pit height. Aluminum poles are more expensive but usually much more durable than the traditional tonkin or "bamboo" type. The life of wood poles can be increased many fold by wrapping strips of tape around the shafts on and between each joint to prevent splitting. (See Fig. 1-13.) Extra large baskets are a very good investment for soft snow.

- *Always use safety straps on your skis.* A runaway ski in deep snow can seldom be found, and a lost ski in the back country can be a disaster. Two short pieces of nylon cord could save your day.

ADVICE TO THE LONELY TOURER

This section contains miscellaneous bits of information that don't fit anywhere else. It includes a few rules of thumb that all tourers should follow, recommendations on how to dress for x-country skiing and suggestions on what items to take on an outing.

- *Never go touring alone.* Regardless of your skiing ability and knowledge of the mountains, accidents sometimes happen. Being stranded alone far from the road with a broken ski or twisted ankle can be fatal in winter.

- Check out the avalanche conditions before attempting a tour which involves that kind of hazard. Information is available from the Forest Service and from people who frequent the back country. By keeping track of the weather for a few days before a tour, you will be more aware of wind and snow conditions. There is no substitute for preparation.

- Tell someone your route, destination, planned time of return, and whom to call if you don't show up. Every hour counts if you're stranded in a storm or buried in an avalanche.

- Dress properly and take extra clothing. A good rule of thumb is to wear several thin layers so things can be

Figure 1-14—Proper dress is vital to the comfort and safety of cross country skiers. It is important not to dress too warmly for climbing, since perspiration causes most fabrics to lose their insulating value. Also, clothing should not be so confining as to restrict the movements of the tourer. (Photo courtesy of O'Dell Peterson.)

removed before perspiration starts. Clothing loses a large percentage of its insulation qualities when it gets wet, particularly cotton. Wool has by far the best properties when damp, so it is hard to beat for ski touring. Wool also absorbs some moisture, which prevents it from getting clammy like many synthetics.

The following list can be used as a guide for selecting clothing to take on a winter outing.

1. A light wool hat with adjustable ear protection.
2. A wool Balaclava-type hat for extended or exposed tours.
3. Sunglasses, preferably with sidepieces to block out glare.
4. A light wool turtle-neck shirt.
5. A wind breaker made of some water and wind repellent

material like nylon or poplin.* Nylon stretch shirts are very comfortable for exercising, but provide very little weather resistance; they are good for short tours or mild temperatures.

6. A warm loose-fitting wool sweater for extended or exposed tours.
7. A warm parka with some kind of hood.
8. Light wool gloves which allow finger movement for fastening bindings and zippers.
9. Warm wool mittens which fit easily over the gloves.
10. Wind and water resistant overmitts for extended or exposed tours.
11. Light wool long-johns.
12. Light wool socks.
13. Warm knee-length wool socks.
14. Wool or poplin knickers, depending upon the duration of the outing and amount of exposure. Stretch nylon knickers are a possibility but have the problem mentioned above.
15. Nylon wind pants. Warm-up pants may be needed with nylon or poplin knickers, but they are too hot and bulky for climbing. The combination of stretch knickers and warm-ups is very effective for short fast climbs with little exposure to severe weather conditions, and long descents in the powder.
16. Gaiters (fabric sleeves that slip over the boots and lower legs to keep out the snow).
17. Boots. A detailed discussion can be found in the previous section on equipment.

When starting out on a tour, the warm parka, mittens, and wind pants can be stuffed in your pack along with the warm hat, overmitts, and sweater. Your shivering won't last long once the climbing starts, but wet clothing caused by wearing your warmest clothes first will keep you cold all day. It is best to take layers off before heating up and to put layers on before cooling down. The warm layers should be saved for lunch stops, changes in weather, and the trip back down the hill. An extra pair of gloves and socks and

---

*Poplin is a tightly woven fabric made of cotton and Dacron. A similar blend of 60/40, cotton/nylon, is quite common and equally good.

Figure 1-15—A pack with provisions for attaching skis can be vital to the ski mountaineer. It is often important to have one's hands free when climbing steep couloirs and ridges on foot, where a dropped ski can be a disaster.

an extra turtle-neck shirt are also a good thing to have in your pack on extended outings in case you do get wet.

- Take enough "stuff" on the tour so you could at least survive any problem that arises. That doesn't mean taking a tent and sleeping bag on a trip around Redman Campground, but dangerous situations can occur even on easy tours when you're a long way from the road. Have enough food and water to last a few extra hours, and warm clothes in case the weather changes. An equipment malfunction or an injury could keep you out longer than planned. Dry socks are a good idea if there's a stream to fall into. A sunburn preventative can sometimes save a great deal of discomfort. One member of the group should have a spare tip for wood skis, band aids for blisters, and tools to take care of equipment problems. (Pliers, screw driver, a spare cable or wire bale where applicable, and some sturdy wire or a roll of fiberglass strapping tape will usually suffice.) These things can easily fit in a small day pack or, for a drier back and better maneuverability, a large fanny pack.

On advanced tours, which involve more time and more

exposure to hazards and weather extremes, it is wise to take an avalanche cord and probe. (An electronic transmitter/receiver is a much better alternative if each member of the group is carrying one.) Matches and a first aid kit should be taken along, and everyone should have plenty of warm clothes. A copy of this book, with topographical maps as a supplement, might certainly come in handy.

A larger pack is obviously needed for advanced tours. Many are available with internal frames to keep them away from the back, and some have side slots or straps for skis. The latter feature is valuable for steep ridges and cornices that must be surmounted on foot.

WASATCH TOURS

The remaining chapters deal with the practicalities of touring in the Wasatch Mountains. Chapter II is a thorough treatment of the subject of avalanches. We cannot overemphasize the hazards that exist in the Wasatch due to extremely heavy snowfalls and extended periods of high wind. It is vital that any tourer who goes into the back country be knowledgeable about avalanche conditions, safe route finding, proper actions if caught in a slide, and rescue procedures.

Tour descriptions commence with Chapter III. That chapter is devoted to areas particularly suited to beginners, and the remaining chapters are divided up geographically. We have tried to list the tours in order of overall difficulty in some chapters, but the reader should be aware that the classification of tours is quite subjective. A person in excellent physical condition, but with little skiing experience, would rate tours very differently from an expert downhill skier who has never climbed a mountain under his own power.

Beginner tours range from outings suitable for anyone, to those requiring a reasonable amount of stamina and skiing ability. Intermediate tours have downhill sections that are steep enough to make it unwise for a novice to attempt them, particularly on light touring equipment. Advanced tours require both endurance and expert skiing skills; and on these, all but the most competent and knowledgeable skiers should use mountaineering or downhill equipment. Super tours speak for themselves. Anyone undertaking one of these marathons needs an intimate knowledge of the mountains and weather, the ability to ski any slope under any snow conditions, the strength to keep going for a full day or longer, and at least a mild case of lunacy. □

2 AVALANCHES

New Year's Eve, 1972. At about 3:00 p.m. in the community of Furnace Creek, two 13 year old boys decided to enjoy the calm at the end of a series of snowstorms. For the past two days it had been snowing, adding eight to twelve inches of fresh snow to an old layer about a foot deep. The boys enjoyed playing snowgames at a nearby ravine. They especially delighted in kicking small cornices off the hillside and watching the blocks of snow roll downward, disintegrating along the way. As they were kicking a cornice a small avalanche released, sweeping the boys downslope and burying them completely. Both died quickly of suffocation in their snowy tombs.

Surprisingly, Furnace Creek is located in upstate New York where one would not expect deep snowfalls and dangerous avalanche conditions. In Utah the combination of sudden and violent winter storms, extended periods of high wind, and snow depths often exceeding 10-15 feet can result in very treacherous avalanche conditions.

Avalanches, or snowslides, are common in Utah. Thousands occur naturally in the mountains every winter and spring. Since the days of the pioneers avalanche accidents and fatalities have also been common in Utah. Over 170 deaths were attributed to this cause in the early mining days when the lust for gold proved stronger than the common sense necessary for winter survival in the Wasatch.

Unlike the mining days, when avalanches involved persons who spent their lives in the mountains—who knew the dangers they faced—today's avalanche victims are usually unsuspecting

33

winter travelers who venture in the nearby mountains mainly for recreation. On February 12, 1967 two young hikers were killed by an avalanche in Pharoah's Glenn just 2 miles from the Mount Olympus Cove subdivision east of Salt Lake City. Another avalanche killed a scout on a February 1968 outing in Rock Canyon near Provo. A research forester, snowmobiling in the foothills above Farmington, was buried by an avalanche during the winter of 1964-1965. Avalanches have claimed lives in the mountains above Ogden and in the foothills near Heber. Even commercial ski areas, where avalanches are meticulously "controlled" by snow-rangers and ski patrols, have had their share of avalanche incidents and fatalities.

Compounding the actual danger of avalanches are many misconceptions harbored by people residing along the Wasatch Front.

"The Greatest Snow on Earth," herald the advertisers "....is found in Utah." Practically from birth, Utahns are taught to adulate snow, to worship "deep powder" and the pleasures it provides. With vast fortunes being spent to promote winter sports, Utahns have been lulled into a state of avalanche apathy: "Powder snow—it's light, it's fluffy, and it's fun; it's harmless."

When an avalanche occurs and a fatality results public apathy is shaken, but only momentarily. Headlines and television vignettes speak of "huge walls of snow", of "giant avalanches", and of "freak winter snowslides". To many avalanche experts such exaggerations are creating the false impression that "large avalanches" are the killers, that "unusual" conditions are necessary or responsible for avalanche fatalities.

Another misunderstanding is the belief that most avalanche victims come out unscathed. This misconception is again perpetuated by news coverage of avalanche accidents. A sudden avalanche (with a resultant fatality) is covered by the press for only a short time. There is, after all, no opportunity to interview the victim. Should an avalanche victim miraculously survive, however, he immediately becomes a hero—complete with feature articles, news editorials, and lengthy personal interviews of his heroic entombment.*

Probably the greatest misconception is the belief that one has to be a skier or a winter mountaineer to be caught in an

---

*A good example of such press coverage is the Dec. 1971 incident at the Snowbird ski complex where a skier was rescued alive after burial in an avalanche for over an hour. So thorough and complete was his post avalanche press coverage that had he been running for public office he would have won by a "landslide."

avalanche. As a group of scouts found out while *hiking* in Rock Canyon near Provo, and as the Farmington snowmobiler discovered, avalanches can happen almost to anyone.

With the continually increasing growth of winter sports such as skiing, snowmobiling, and cross-country touring, it is important that the public residing along the highly populated Wasatch Front becomes aware of the dangers of avalanches that exist in the mountains so near their homes.

This chapter deals with these dangers in general terms. It covers the conditions that may lead to avalanches, ways to avoid them and describes tactics one should employ to increase his chances of survival if he is unfortunate enough to be engulfed by one. It is hoped that misconceptions held by back country users will be dispelled and better safety practices will be observed.

A novice tourer is not expected to learn immediately all the avalanche evaluation characteristics and techniques mentioned in this chapter. Nor will he have access to all pertinent data necessary for such analyses. In the vicinity of commercial ski areas along the Wasatch Front the Salt Lake Ranger District of the Wasatch National Forest can provide the backcountry traveler with much valuable avalanche advice. Most of this information is based on data gathered as part of avalanche control activities at nearby ski resorts. Some of it is based on reports of interested and knowledgeable ski touring parties. The forest service avalanche condition reports are only advisory in nature, but you should take their recommendations seriously unless you are certain that your information is more complete.†

The Cold Facts of Avalanches

"The best avalanche...is someone else's," remarked the member of a local touring group who had been involved in a recent avalanche. In preparation for a season of safe ski touring, snowshoeing, or snowmobiling, everyone should become familiar with other people's avalanche misfortunes. Enough avalanche burials have occurred in the United States over the past thirty years to warrant compilation and publication by the United States Forest Service of two volumes of avalanche case histories. These are entitled *THE SNOWY TORRENTS: Avalanche*

---

†The U.S. Forest Service is currently experimenting with a regional avalanche forecasting system. These reports may become part of weather, news, or sports broadcasts on local radio and television stations.

Accidents in the United States, 1910–1966 and *THE SNOWY TORRENTS: Avalanche Accidents in the United States, 1967–1971.* These volumes contain some interesting avalanche histories, both in the back country and at some of the major ski resorts.

Two other publications which provide valuable information are the United States Forest Service *AVALANCHE HANDBOOK,* written by Ronald I. Perla and M. Martinelli Jr. and the *ABC's of AVALANCHE SAFETY,* written by E. R. LaChapelle, one of the top avalanche authorities in the U.S. While the *Avalanche Handbook* contains mostly techniques and procedures to be followed by avalanche personnel of highway departments, ski areas, and the Forest Service, it also contains some excellent details concerning avalanche hazard formation and evaluation. Chapter eight of the "Handbook" is must reading for the ski tourer since it deals primarily with back country avalanches, the statistics of survival, route selection, and finally avalanche rescue and first aid. All three of the Forest Service texts are available to the public.*

What are the facts concerning avalanches that should be learned by all tourers?

- Back country accidents account for the largest number of avalanche fatalities in North America. The victims are usually ski tourers, helicopter skiers, or mountaineers. Snowmobilers and hikers are becoming more frequently involved in avalanche fatalities.

- After one half hour of burial, the victim's chances of surviving is only about 50 percent. This fact should be kept in mind by the members of a ski touring party when one of their companions has been buried by a slide. They must consider his decreased chances of survival if they abandon him to go for help. The grim statistics of burial time and survival probability are tabulated in Fig. 2–1.

- Less than 20 percent of the victims buried completely (with no trace showing) have been found alive. This leads

---

*Persons may obtain the *Avalanche Handbook* from the Government Printing Office in Washington, D.C. In ordering please ask for *USDA Forest Service Agricultural Handbook No. 489* by R. I. Perla and M. Martinelli, Jr. The 1967–1971 volume of *The Snowy Torrents* should be ordered as: *USDA Forest Service General Technical Report RM-8 (March, 1975)* by Knox Williams.

A few copies of the 1910–1966 *Snowy Torrents* are available from the "Alpine Snow and Avalanche Research Project," Rocky Mountain Forest and Range Experiment Station, 240 West Prospect Street, Fort Collins, Colorado 80521.

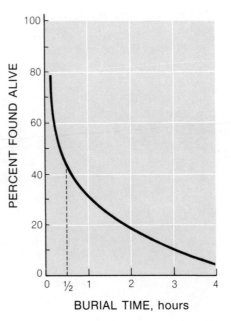

Figure 2-1 — Based on 82 avalanche rescues in the USA scientists have formulated this survival probability chart. Note that after ½ hour of burial a victim's chance of being alive is only 50%. Chances of surival decrease thereafter.

to the conclusion that a victim's best chance of survival depends on having an arm, a leg, or ski thrust out from the avalanche as he is being buried.

- Most avalanche fatalities are due to suffocation. This point completely negates the popular misconception that there is a lot of air in the snow for the victim to breathe. "In a typical avalanche burial," write the authors of the "Handbook," "there is rather little air trapped in pore space around the victim, and it is only a matter of time until the victim loses consciousness and dies. The weight of snow bears down on the victim's throat and chest and further accelerates respiratory failure." Broken necks, or backs, or legs, head injuries, or abdominal injuries are also common among avalanche victims who have been swept down in snowslides.

- The most dangerous avalanches are those released by the victim himself. Staying off a potential avalanche slope is the best protection against entrapment by an avalanche.

- "Small avalanches are the killers," is the message of importance in both volumes of *The Snowy Torrents*. "Almost

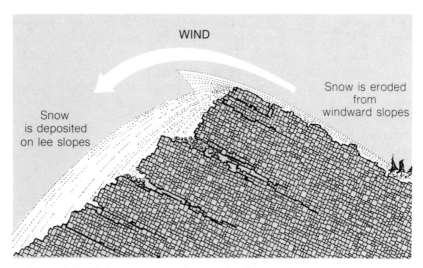

WIND

Snow is eroded from windward slopes

Snow is deposited on lee slopes

Figure 2-2—Wind can move great amounts of snow, frequently creating severe avalanche hazards on lee slopes, where heavy deposition occurs. Windward slopes may be safer although tourers should watch for isolated pockets of wind slab even in these areas.

50 percent of the fatal accidents resulted from slides which ran less than 100 meters (300 ft)."†

Types of Avalanches

In order for an avalanche to occur there must be snow, a slope on which the snow can slide, and some form of instability setting the snow in motion. Snow can be set in motion in a number of ways, most commonly by collapse of a weak layer underneath, by snow falling from above, or even by the weight of a skier moving along the surface.

There are two basic types of avalanche, loose snow and slab. Loose snow avalanches are characterized by a surface layer of snow that is not bonded together very well. Loose snow avalanches often occur soon after a heavy fall of dry snow. Immediately after a storm, danger is greatest, but it decreases with time as the snow consolidates. The lower the temperature,

---

†A recent tragedy occurred in downtown Toronto, Canada, where two girls, tobogganing in a city park, were killed by an avalanche only 6 feet wide and several hundred feet long. The volume of snow in which they were buried was approximately equal to that of a large city bus.

the longer the stabilization process takes. For example, consolidation may require only a few days at 20°, but could take weeks at subzero temperatures. This is one reason that cold north-facing slopes present such a great danger in winter.

Another type of loose snow avalanche is the wet snow slide that usually occurs in the spring. Rain or warm temperatures soften the snow and saturate it with water, thus weakening the internal bonds between the crystals. This condition leads to some of the most devastating avalanches due to the excessive weight of water-saturated snow.

Slab avalanches frequently occur in areas where the wind has built up a compact layer of snow that has not adhered sufficiently to that which is below. As illustrated in Fig. 2-2 leeward slopes are usually more prone to slab formation than windward slopes. This condition also stabilizes in time, but a hazard can last for extended periods, particularly if temperatures are low. This situation is potentially the most dangerous; a slab can remain in place for long periods of time and then be released when it is disturbed by passage of a touring party.

TO TOUR OR NOT TO TOUR?

"To tour or not to tour?" From the first winter snowfall, and throughout the ski touring season, that is the question. Each weekend from November through May groups of tourers, or individuals, struggle with the decision-making process of whether or not to tour on a particular day. Most Utah tourers, especially novices, are not equipped with the knowledge necessary for wise decision-making in avalanche terrain.

There are four basic types of information that must be considered before undertaking any tour.

- Prior weather and snow history.
- Characteristics of the terrain.
- Current weather and snow conditions.
- The touring party.

The remainder of this section is devoted to a discussion of these items and their usefullness in assuring a safe and successful outing.

Prior Weather and Snow History.

A proficient tourer should become familiar with weather and snow patterns for the entire season. He should especially note the following details:

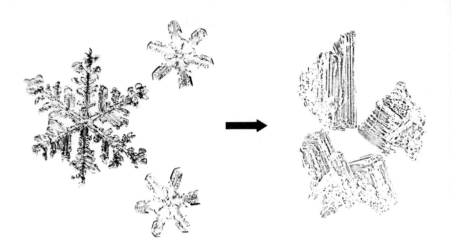

Figure 2-3—Periods of cold weather, aided by heat from the earth, can transform "regular" snowflakes (as shown at left) into larger granules known as "depth hoar" (illustrated at right). A layer of such hoar particles can cause avalanche hazards which may persist for months.

EARLY SEASON SNOWSTORMS.   In the Wasatch mountains early snowstorms are often the cause of severe avalanche conditions throughout the entire season. October storms frequently deposit several feet of snow. On south and west facing slopes it usually melts off fairly quickly. On north and east facing slopes, however, the snow persists. As it sits there during long periods of cold weather, chemical changes can take place within individual snowflakes. As illustrated schematically in Fig. 2-3, this chemical transformation can change branched and interlocked, star-like crystals into smoother granules commonly called "depth hoar." Such hoar granules can act like ball bearings underneath any new snow falling later in the year.

PROLONGED COLD OR WARM SPELLS.   As mentioned above prolonged cold may cause formation of depth hoar early in the season. Warming of hoar granules, however, may weld them together into a more stable mass. An extended period of very cold weather after a heavy snowstorm can cause unstable conditions to last indefinitely.

LARGE SNOW ACCUMULATIONS.   It is not too unusual in the Wasatch Mountains to receive snowfalls of 30 to 60 inches during one severe blizzard. Such deep snow accumulations should be regarded with extreme caution and touring should not be attempted until several days (or even weeks) have passed allowing natural consolidation of the snow.*

WIND. High winds accompanying and/or following a snowstorm can very quickly develop dangerous slab conditions. Often the air is calm in Salt Lake Valley, but snow plumes can be observed off the nearby summits. This is a warning signal to watch for on days preceding a tour.

SURFACE UNDER LAST SNOWFALL. All things being equal, rougher surfaces will hold new snow best. Thus, early in the season when rocks, bushes, and tree stumps protrude far enough to cause irregularities in the snow, new snow is less likely to slide. Later on, however, when the snow is deep enough to cover these terrain features, it is more likely to slide. It is helpful to know the nature of the ski touring area in summertime, particularly if there are any smooth rock slabs, areas of grassy slopes, etc. that could be hazardous throughout the winter.

RAINS. Rains may fall onto a snowpack creating a hard, glass-like ice crust. Future snowfalls may, or may not, bond very well to such ice crusts depending upon temperature conditions that prevail before and during the storm. Also, wet snow avalanche mentioned previously can be released by rain percolating through the snow, destroying its cohesion, and lubricating underlying snow or rock layers.

LATE SEASON SNOWSTORMS. Late season snowfalls are also common in the Wasatch Mountains. If a surface crust has formed before the storm, severe avalanche conditions can result. Even though depth of such new snowfalls can be less than 6 inches, the severity of these avalanches can be great. Many small slopes can slide simultaneously and converge in narrow gullies. Hundreds of such snowslides were observed east of Bountiful and Farmington on a recent spring flight along the foothills of the Wasatch. Two such avalanches are illustrated in Fig. 2–4.

Characteristics of the Terrain.

The physical aspects of the terrain that is to be traversed during a ski tour is the second most important consideration in

---

*During the early 1960's one storm—resulting from the collision of an arctic cold front with a moist Gulf of Mexico airmass—dropped about 100 inches of snow at and near Alta. Over a hundred avalanches crossed the Little Cottonwood Canyon road. Avalanche conditions were so severe that aircraft traffic was banned from the area (noise!) and all guests and residents of Alta lodges were evacuated by snowcat into Salt Lake Valley.

Figure 2-4—Although the fracture lines of these avalanches are only 4 inches thick the large area involved in these spring slides, could be fatal to anyone passing beneath. (In the Pharoah's Glen avalanche two hikers were killed by a slide which had only a 4 inch fracture line.)

the decision-making process. A number of factors are critical to analysis of ski touring terrain.

STEEPNESS. Generally, the steeper the terrain, the greater the avalanche hazard. Avalanches can be triggered most easily on slopes of 30° to 50° inclination. They very rarely start on inclines of less than 25°, but tourers must remember that avalanches can run out onto terrain that is flat or even uphill.

WIND EXPOSURE. Wind can move great amounts of snow from one area to another. Such drifting can cause regions of deep snow accumulation making some places quite hazardous. This type of danger is illustrated in Fig. 2–5, a photograph showing an actual slab avalanche which resulted from such a snow accumulation. Wind also forms cornices which may collapse, crushing skiers underneath or starting a serious avalanche.

EXPOSURE TO SUN. If a slope is exposed to the warming rays of the sun for extended periods an icy crust may form. New snow falling on such a crust may tend to avalanche easily. Prolonged exposure to sun may also cause weakening of a snow layer, particularly in the spring. Experienced tourers try to avoid sunbaked slopes throughout the afternoon, when greatest melting takes place. The sun sometimes helps to stabilize snow after a storm. New powder consolidates more quickly on south and west facing slopes where temperatures are higher. This process can often be observed around trees, where cones form

Figure 2-5—Prevailing winds have deposited vast amounts of snow below a ridge of Mount Timpanogos. One slope has avalanched, leaving an easily visible fracture line 2-3 feet thick.

around trunks as a result of settling.

TIMBER. Avalanches occur in timbered areas as well as on open slopes, but forested slopes (if the timber is sufficiently dense) can provide some protection. As a simple rule: "if trees are spaced just close enough from each other to make ski travel through them annoying" the protection offered by the trees is "adequate."

TOPOGRAPHICAL FEATURES. The Wasatch Mountains possess some unusual topographical features which can increase considerably the danger on some tours. In some areas of Big and Little Cottonwood canyons sheer slabs of rock thrust out at an angle of about 25°. These slabs are not sufficiently steep to eliminate all avalanche hazard as the snow falls during a storm. Deep snowslides can accumulate on such rock formations later releasing to cause considerable damage. Frequently such slab areas are located along popular ski tour routes. Two are illustrated in Fig. 2-6.

Hanging valleys and steep, high, slopes ending in narrow ravines and gullies are other characteristic features in the

Figure 2-6—Quartzite slabs near Lake Blanche. Left photo shows rock slab early in the season. Photo at right shows similar rock slabs with accumulation of snow. Passing beneath such snow-laden rock slabs is a certain invitation to disaster.

Wasatch that should be viewed with suspicion by the careful tourer. Two examples are shown in Fig. 2–7.

DISTANCE AND ELEVATION CHANGES.   These parameters are important because they demand forethought on the part of the touring party. Snow conditions can vary drastically as a function of elevation and location in the Wasatch. While it may be very warm at the 6,500 ft. level, it may be freezing cold at 10,000 ft. Totally different avalanche conditions exist at these different elevations. The distance and elevation change of a ski tour also directly affect physical fatigue of the tourers. The longer the tour and the more exhausted the participants, the more likely they are to have impaired judgment.

Current Weather and Snow Conditions.

SEASON.   Each season and each mountain range has its peculiarities. During early season (usually November through February in the Wasatch) the winter snowpack may be unstable

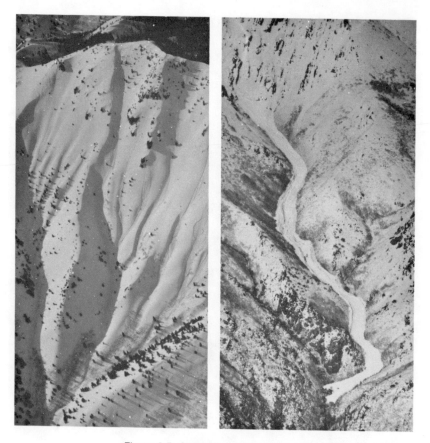

Figure 2-7—In the Wasatch Mountains there are many small canyons which terminate in steep, high slopes as shown at left. Such slopes can channel great amounts of snow into narrow, winding, gullies as shown at right. Under proper conditions such gullies can become death traps to unsuspecting ski tourers or snowmobilers.

due to lack of consolidation. Between February and April the snowpack is in process of consolidation and touring can be good if conducted with caution.

Late season touring is safest since avalanches occur on more predictable schedules. During early morning the snow is icy, hard, and good for travel. By late morning east-facing slopes begin to soften and avalanching can occur. West-facing areas are slower to warm, so they may be safe for an extra hour or two. Near sunset things start to freeze again and tend to stabi-

Figure 2-8—Water percolating under the snowpack can act
as a lubricant on which snow will slide. This photo illustrates
an extremely hazardous avalanche area in upper Broads Fork,
Big Cottonwood Canyon.

lize. The implications are obvious: Be off the mountain by noon, or take a very long summit siesta!

TEMPERATURE. The temperature of snow and surrounding air is a very complex parameter in the study of avalanches. Penetration of heat into a snowpack can have very different effects. As mentioned previously it can consolidate an unstable slope after a winter storm. However, penetration of excessive heat may cause melting of individual snow crystals and percolation of water through the snow to underlying surfaces such as rocks, grass, or other snow. Water between layers of snow or between the snow-rock surface may act as a lubricant on which avalanches occur. Such lubrication of underlying rock strata are shown in Fig. 2–8.

SNOW CONDITIONS. The depth of new snow can be an excellent indicator of possible instability. If a tourer easily sinks over his knees in powder the snow is obviously unconsolidated and weak. A powder avalanche may easily be triggered by a skier. Deep powder is not the only prerequisite for a snow slide, however. Slab conditions may be just as hazardous. If a tourer notices cracks forming in the snow in front of his skis as he moves, he should consider returning to a safer area. Movement and noise can often be detected in a slab as it settles around a touring party. These are definite indications of instability.

UNDERLYING SNOW LAYERS. Professional avalanche workers dig deep pits (often to ground level) to study the composition of individual snow layers. This is usually impractical for ski tourers, but one can get a "semiqualitative" feeling of a snowpack by thrusting an inverted ski pole deep into the snow. If the pole penetrates evenly with some resistance, then suddenly shows no resistance, there may be a weak layer underneath. This is by no means a foolproof method of detecting an unstable snow condition and tourers should always suspect an avalanche on uncompacted slopes.

SIGNS OF RECENT AVALANCHE ACTIVITY. Much information can be gained by a tourer before he enters an avalanche prone area simply by observing slopes of similar exposure. If any recent avalanche activity is evident, care should be exercised. In spring a telltale sign of potential danger is formation of snowballs at the base of rocks. When snowballs begin small slides (Fig. 2–9) or become quite large as they roll downward, watch out!

47

Figure 2-9—Snowballs tend to form on spring days as the rocks warm in the sun and the snow slides off. These can be a danger signal.

The Touring Party

PHYSICAL CONDITION/EXPERIENCE OF MEMBERS. An experienced tourer can move quickly and confidently over all types of terrain encountered on a ski tour. If one member of a ski touring group is physically weaker or less experienced than the others, he can cause delays in areas where speed is essential or otherwise jeopardize group safety. A good tour leader will consider the ability of the group as a whole and choose a route that is safe and enjoyable for all.

NUMBER OF TOURERS IN PARTY. After only one half hour of burial an avalanche victim's chance of survival is only about 50 percent. This suggests that a larger touring party could be more effective in a possible rescue. However, too many people on a ski tour can be difficult to keep together. Sometimes one portion of a large group can expose others to avalanche hazard. After years of touring in the Wasatch the authors feel that a party of 4 to 7 persons is about optimum.

KNOWLEDGE OF TERRAIN. Good knowledge of terrain can help avoid avalanche incidents. To an unsuspecting tourer a particular route may look safe, but better familiarity with the surrounding terrain may prove the contrary. A steep slab of

Figure 2-10—Two touring parties (routes 1 and 2) have been involved in separate avalanches while approaching a popular mountain pass in the Wasatch. Knowing this, can the reader find an "avalanche proof" route to this pass? After puzzling over this same problem, several avalanche experts have concluded that "...there is simply no safe route across this cirque."

snow, or an overloaded cornice may be poised, ready to release, several hundred yards above the tourers.

Most of the intermediate and advanced ski tours in the Wasatch cross at least one known avalanche path. Some of these paths slide frequently, others only seldom. Knowing where the most dangerous paths lay may suggest changes in a proposed route, or under certain circumstances cancellation of a tour. Fig. 2-10 illustrates the usefulness of prior avalanche his-

49

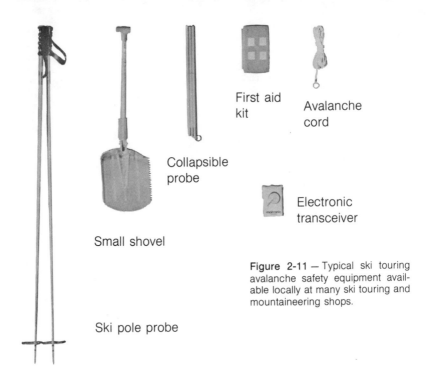

First aid kit

Avalanche cord

Collapsible probe

Electronic transceiver

Small shovel

Figure 2-11 — Typical ski touring avalanche safety equipment available locally at many ski touring and mountaineering shops.

Ski pole probe

tory in ski tour planning and route selection.

PARTY ENTHUSIASM. The level of "enthusiasm" can be a contributing factor in avalanche safety. Here is what the authors of the *Avalanche Handbook* say of party enthusiasm:

> "Back country safety is first of all a matter of controlling enthusiasm. In the spirit of adventure, many accidents occur because even the most experienced ski mountaineer may take what he thinks is a small risk to reach his objective. This enthusiasm is reinforced by the psychological feeling of group security that comes when several people push forward together—no single member of the group likes to admit concern and turn the party around prematurely."

FIRST AID AND RESCUE CAPABILITY. In event of accident, good, clear thinking, quick and confident action with proper equipment are necessary. These do not come naturally, but have to be learned and practiced.* Each member of a well prepared group should carry either a collapsible probe, or ski

_____

*Several local outing clubs—primarily the Wasatch Mountain Club of Salt Lake City—conduct annual avalanche rescue practice sessions for interested tourers.

poles convertible to probes. New electronic detectors have proven very effective if most members of the party have them. A personal first aid kit is mandatory. An avalanche cord, to be worn on dangerous terrain, is a good investment also. The party should have a small, lightweight snow shovel for digging out a buried companion since skis or ski tips do not work well or often not at all in the hard snow of avalanche debris. In Colorado a buried ski tourer, who was quickly located by an electronic detector, died because his companions could not dig down to him quickly enough through hard snow 8 feet deep without a shovel.

CLOTHING AND TOURING EQUIPMENT. Proper clothing becomes very important in event of an avalanche and burial. The victim is usually in shock and needs extra warmth to help preserve his life. Extra clothing carried by companions will aid a victim during evacuation or in event of a bivouac.

ON WITH THE SKI TOUR!

You've kissed your roommate goodby, and now you're on your way. Whether you return alive and well, or whether you are buried, injured, or killed by an avalanche depends on either your selection of an absolutely safe ski tour route, or more likely on how you handle slopes with some degree of avalanche hazard. There are a number of trails in the Wasatch which have little or no avalanche exposure. Such terrain is usually located in canyon bottoms, along gently sloping streams, or in the heavily wooded areas that make up much of the local canyons. There are also many ridges which can be toured in relative safety. Unless a particular cross-country tour intersects the runout zones of higher avalanches it can be considered safe if its slope is less than 15°. Beginning tourers are especially fortunate here, for most of their ski touring terrain is usually safe.

Route Finding

Nearly all terrain available for intermediate and advanced touring is, at one time or another, likely to avalanche. The degree of exposure to avalanche hazard varies from tour to tour. Some intermediate ski tours cross only an occasional, moderately dangerous slope, others may cross many consecutive slopes, all prone to slide under the proper conditions.

Figure 2-12—An example of gentle, sloping ridges which are suitable for touring or snowmobiling. Althouth this photo was taken along the foothills above Farmington, there are similar areas throughout the Wasatch Range.

With knowledge that some avalanche slopes have to be crossed it is the tour leader's responsibility to select the safest possible route. Unfortunately choosing the safest possible route is not always done with total objectivity. Like auto racing, ski touring has its risks and its rewards. Too often, the tour leader's judgment is slanted toward the "reward" side with little or no consideration being given to the "risks" involved. Even more unfortunately, many tour leaders learn their touring and route selection techniques by following long established "patterns"— patterns that have evolved over a period of time with little consideration to avalanche safety.

To help potential leaders locate safe touring routes some guide lines have been proposed by the Forest Service and are briefly repeated here:

- The safest routes are on top of ridges, preferably on the windward side, and in canyon bottoms, far out from any avalanche paths.

Figure 2-13—A popular ski touring route to Cardiff Pass is illustrated in this photograph. It is common practice for unwary tourers to follow the dotted line among open slopes to reach Cardiff Pass. This route exposes them to a large avalanche shown in the photo above. A safer route would lead them through the trees at the right. (Photo courtesy of Dr. R.I. Perla.)

- Heavily wooded areas can offer some protection, but are not guaranteed safe, particularly if avalanche slopes lie above.
- When climbing fairly steep slopes, try to stay on ridges or other prominences which could deflect or channel an avalanche away from your party.
- If you have to cross a suspected avalanche path, stay as high as possible so that if a slide does occur, you will be on top. Be sure that the slide path does not end in a narrow gully (where you could be buried deeply) or that it does not cascade over cliffs or other obstructions (where you could be injured by impact with objects, etc.)
- When you must ascend a known avalanche zone keep to the flanks and edges, and climb straight up rather than traversing back and forth.

Several other, somewhat technical guide lines are also described in the *Avalanche Handbook,* but will not be repeated here. Figure 2–13 illustrates a typical route selection problem along the Cardiff Pass touring route. Both "poor" (dotted line) and "safer" routes (solid line) are shown.

Precautions in Avalanche Terrain.

In addition to being properly equipped (with rescue equipment, first aid kits, etc.) there are several precautions that a ski touring party should take if it becomes necessary to cross a hazardous slope.

- Only one person at a time should be exposed. Others in the party should remain at a safe location where they can watch each member as he crosses the slope. Each remaining member then takes his turn to cross the slope individually. It should not be assumed that the remainder of the whole party can now cross safely just because one, two, or three skiers have crossed it individually. The first person to cross may just disturb the slope enough that it could be released by subsequent skiers. Fig. 2–14 illustrates this possibility in two frames from a spectacular 8mm motion picture sequence taken by co-author David Zapruder Hanscom.

- Remove ski pole wrist loops and ski safety straps. If a victim's hands and feet are free his chances of survival are increased, since he will have more freedom of movement as he is being buried.

- Clothing. Before entering a slope clothing should be buttoned, parka hood should be donned, mittens and wind pants or warmups worn. These items help insulate the victim from the snow in event of burial.

- Personal escape route. As a skier starts across an avalanche route he should search out, and keep in mind, possible escape routes to the flank to be used if an avalanche starts above him or if he triggers a slide himself.

- Fast movement. For obvious reasons tourers should not linger on a potential avalanche slope.

- Electronic transceiver. If electronic rescue devices are used, they should be checked to be sure they are turned on and in the transmit mode.

- Avalanche cord. Some tourers choose to trail a long, lightweight, orange or red cord behind them as they cross a

Figure 2-14—The photographer and three others had just crossed a known avalanche slope and were preparing to lunch atop "Cardiac Pass" near Alta. As skiers numbered 5, 6, and 7 approached the pass, a small avalanche (A) was triggered beneath the track of skier 5. The top frame shows the large fracture resulting from this slide. With renewed enthusiasm, skier 5 hastily advanced to a safer location closer to the pass.

While the camera was still running (bottom frame) a larger avalanche (B) suddenly released, trapping and sweeping skiers 6 and 7 to the bottom of the runout zone some 1200 feet downslope. Note in the lower frame the great extent of the second fracture line.

Figure 2-15—Immediately after a back country avalanche in Big Cottonwood Canyon two tourers rush to the aid of a partially buried companion indicated by arrow. Had he been buried completely, his avalanche cord, easily visible in the foreground, may have led to a speedy rescue.

slope. If caught and buried in an avalanche, they claim, the cord may remain unburied or easily located in a preliminary search thus leading rescuers quickly to the victim. Such an avalanche cord is visible in Fig. 2-15, a photograph taken just seconds after four persons were swept down in a back-country avalanche. Avalanche cords, however, are not totally reliable—some have been buried completely alongside their owners.

RUMBLE, ROAR, AND RESCUE.

A number of Utahns have been caught in avalanches and have survived. Their experiences and their impressions at the "moment of truth" are revealing and instructional for would-be Wasatch tourers.

"I heard this rumble," recalls a 13-year-old scout involved in a fatal avalanche in Rock Canyon near Provo. "It was a big noise—pretty loud. I looked back of us and saw this big mass of snow coming. It was bumping and flying over the rocks higher above us." His assistant scoutmaster, age 29, had a similar recollection of the incident. "I first heard a noise like a jet aircraft overhead but saw nothing. The next thing I felt was the snow engulfing me. I swam like crazy just trying to keep my arms and legs from being trapped." The assistant scoutmaster was buried to his chest in snow. One of his scouts was killed in this unfortunate accident.

Dr. R. I. Perla, an experienced Snow Ranger for the Wasatch National Forest recalls his miraculous escape as he was swept 1,500 feet down one of the "Baldy Chutes" in a large avalanche at Alta.

"The cornice broke...and I was in the chute. I knew it was a large avalanche and I tried to make swimming motions to stay on top. The force of the snow against my face closed my eyes. The amount of time I was in motion seemed to go by quickly, and I sensed coming to rest...I realized I was face up. I tried to place my left hand over my face, but the piling up snow forced it away....Before the snow set up, I was successful in getting my right hand up through the snow...I knew my hand was out of the snow and that I had excellent chances. I then tried to conserve air awaiting rescue, but almost immediately blacked out." His outstretched hand led several area skiers to him and he was dug out and revived in less than 3 minutes!

By studying and analyzing avalanche survivals such as these, researchers have evolved a number of suggestions that should become "instinctive" in the soul of every tourer and winter recreationist.

Actions by an Avalanche Victim

PICKING OUT AN ESCAPE ROUTE. When an avalanche starts around and above a victim, his best chance of survival is to escape out to a side by skiing along with the moving snow. This reaction should be instantaneous. If the avalanche occurs beneath his ski track (such as in the upper frame of Figure 2–14) he should attempt to hold his position above the slide.

SWIMMING. If it is not possible to ski out of the avalanche or stay above it, the victim should get rid of his skis and poles and make "swimming" motions to help work his way to the side. In both the Rock Canyon and the Baldy "chute" avalanches, as well as in many other avalanche cases in the U.S., victims avoided deep burial by using a swimming motion as they were being swept down in the snow. A "breast-stroke" is recommended for victims being carried downhill head-first; a "treading water" motion for those being carried downhill feet-first.

THRUSTING A HAND UP. Many victims owe their life to having a hand thrust above the snow at the moment of burial.

FORMING A BREATHING SPACE. To prevent snow from entering the mouth and other breathing passages the victim should use one arm to form an "air pocket" around his face as he is being engulfed. The "research forester" mentioned in the introduction to this chapter may owe his life to such an air pocket that he was able to form with his arm. He survived complete burial for four hours before being rescued.

CONSERVING OXYGEN. In order to conserve oxygen, the victim should relax and not fight the sensation to black out. Energy should not be wasted struggling. Shouting for help may be of no use unless the rescuers are very near.

Rescue Procedure.

Once totally buried, the victim's chance of survival passes into the hands of his companions. How instinctively, how quickly, how expertly and confidently they perform the search and rescue will determine his remaining longevity.

Because the victim's best chance (a chance greater than 50:50) of survival is to be rescued in the first 30 minutes or less it is usually inadvisable to send a messenger for help. In most back-country in the Wasatch it would take a competent messenger at least 30–60 minutes to ski for help. If the touring party is small every member is better used at the accident site. Cases have been documented where a companion has left the scene of an avalanche and returned a few hours later with an organized rescue party, only to find the victim is already dead, but with a portion of his body, or a piece of equipment sticking out of the snow.

What should the survivors do to locate a buried companion? A number of quickly and efficiently performed steps are recommended by the Forest Service:

- Analyze avalanche danger from any adjacent slopes. Post an avalanche guard if necessary and plan an escape route from any additional avalanches threatening the rescue.

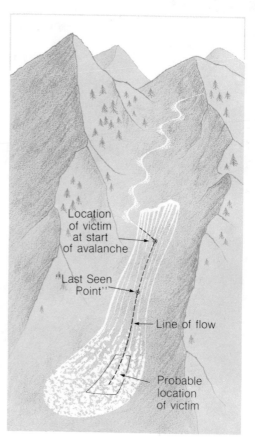

Figure 2-16—If two points of a victim's trajectory can be established, a high probability exists that the victim will be near the downhill flow line passing through these two points. (Illustration courtesy of "Alpine Snow and Avalanche Project" —U.S. Forest Service)

- Point of entry. Ski tracks or observation of witnesses can usually establish the location of the victim at the start of the avalanche. This spot should be marked with a ski or pole.
- Last seen point. Determine as best you can the "last seen point," the point at which the victim disappeared beneath the snow. This should also be marked with a ski pole or ski.
- Determine possible trajectory. The line between the point of entry and the last-seen point should lead to the location of the victim as illustrated in Figure 2–16. Items of equipment may also be scattered along this line and may sometimes end up quite close to the victim.
- Determine the region of "highest priority search." This area will be determined by clues, or, as illustrated in Fig.

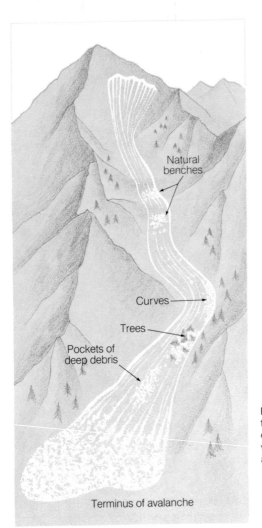

Natural
benches

Curves

Trees

Pockets of
deep debris

Terminus of avalanche

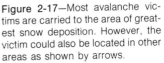

Figure 2-17—Most avalanche victims are carried to the area of greatest snow deposition. However, the victim could also be located in other areas as shown by arrows.

2-17, may include deep areas of snow debris, the terminus of the avalanche, areas between trees where a victim may have been trapped, or snow depositions near natural "benches" or in curves of the avalanche path.

- Make a rapid, but systematic search of the surface of the debris in the regions of highest priority. Mark all clues. The greatest probability of a live rescue is in this initial "surface-search" operation, where a searcher may spot a hand, an avalanche cord, or some other part of the buried skier.

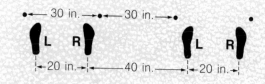

Line
advances
one step
(approx. 2 ft.)

30 in. → 30 in.

L R   L R

20 in. ← 40 in. → 20 in.

Figure 2-18—Execution of a coarse probe when the number of probers is limited. Although such "coarse" probing gives only about a 70% chance of finding the victim its high speed maximizes the probability of *finding the victim alive.*

PROBING.   If the surface search in the most probable areas has failed to locate the victim, a "probe line" is established to try to locate the victim with skis, ski poles, or collapsible avalanche probes. There are two methods of probing for victims. The "coarse" probe (poles inserted approximately every 2½ feet) or the "fine" probe (every foot). Coarse probing is used whenever there is any hope of finding a victim alive and is best suited for immediate back-country searches by small parties. The best procedure is to make several passes using the coarse probing technique, until the victim is found. Fig. 2–18 shows how "coarse" probing is executed.

1. Probers line up finger tip to finger tip, arms extended, feet about 2 feet apart.
2. Two probe insertions are made in the snow, once to the left of the prober's body, once to the right.
3. On command from a designated leader the line advances one step (about 2½ feet) and repeats the right and left probe insertions.
4. Strict discipline, clear and firm commands, a rhythm assuring maximum pace are essential.
5. Except for the leader's commands total silence should be observed by the probers. In two Utah back-country avalanche rescues a victim was located by his shouting for help to his rescuers above.

The probe line advances upslope. If a possible "strike" of the victim is made, one person drops out of the line to investigate by digging or further probing. The remainder of the line keep advancing and probing.

First Aid and Revival.

When the victim has been located and partially dug out, first aid procedures must be started immediately. All tourers should be familiar with Red Cross procedures so the proper actions can be taken as quickly as possible.

Unless an avalanche victim has been swept over cliffs or has been "strained" through closely spaced trees it is unlikely that he will be bleeding profusely. If he is, immediate priority must be to stop the bleeding.

It is very likely that the victim of an avalanche will not be breathing. Next priority, therefore, must be to restore breathing. The victim need not be completely dug out for start of artificial respiration, only his face need be exposed. Mouth-to-mouth resuscitation is started as soon as his breathing passages are cleared of snow or other matter. When these things are accomplished, minor wounds can be bandaged and suspected broken bones immobilized.

If the victim is able to ski out he should do so immediately to allow as much time as possible should problems develop. If help is required to transport him to civilization another member of the group can remain with the victim to be sure he is warm and comfortable.

Avalanches—Easily Avoided, Rarely Survived.

The lesson to be learned by ski tourers from a study of avalanche information is very simple: be informed about weather and snow conditions and use a great deal of discretion as to when and where to tour. It is better to take a longer route, or to do a less exposed ski tour, or even to stay at home, if there is any doubt about safety.

The statistics of survival of avalanche victims speak for themselves. The risk is simply too great. □

Photo courtesy Richard Armstrong, *Institute of Arctic and Alpine Research.*

Jack McLellan Photo

3 BEGINNER TOURS

Ski touring in the Wasatch Mountains is very different from skiing over the traditional hard-packed ski tracks in rolling terrain. Most of our touring is done in canyons which are generally uphill in one direction and down in the other. This means that a skier must soon learn to be comfortable sliding downhill on touring skis or be confined to flat terrain, such as Big Cottonwood Canyon around Brighton and Solitude or the Park City golf course.

Ski touring is made easier in the Wasatch by the large quantity of light powder snow. Its consistent texture enables the novice to stay under control and helps him to master skiing techniques. Many beginners are able to handle some of the intermediate tours by the end of their first full season.

The blessing of large quantities of powder snow brings with it the very real hazard of avalanches. There is little danger on any of the beginner tours, but anyone venturing into the Wasatch Mountains in the winter must be aware of his surroundings at all times. A steep bank or short slope above the trail can appear harmless but might slide upon a tourer. Other skiers high up on the side of the canyon could set off a major avalanche that could involve people on the otherwise safe terrain below. One cannot be too careful.

One problem that should be mentioned about gentle touring terrain is the noisy nemesis of winter solitude, the snow machine.

65

The areas described in this chapter are relatively free of the beasts, but skiing in heavily used locations, such as the Guardsman's Pass road, lower Cardiff Fork, or lower American Fork, can be very unpleasant. Snowmobiles are also allowed in Millcreek, Mill F, Mill D, Silver Fork, and Redman Campground, but they are usually not too numerous. It should be noted that very few of them have been observed on the trail before ten o'clock, so an early start will often prevent any encounter.

WHERE TO START

After reading the first two chapters of this book, the beginner tourer has undoubtedly rented some equipment but is too terrified of avalanches to venture into the mountains. So where does he go to develop some confidence and skiing skills? Preferably he will start on flat terrain that is far from any hazard and take along an experienced tourer who can provide some guidance. One logical approach is to participate in one or more of the clinics or lessons run by various ski shops and ski schools in Salt Lake City and Park City. Expert instruction is available to anyone for little or no money.

When basic ski touring technique has been mastered, the beginner needs to find places to enjoy his new activity. He is limited only by his imagination at this point, but there are several possibilities to consider.

- Many golf courses are high enough to be snow-covered during part of the winter. Bonneville, Mountain Dell, Park City and Wasatch State Park are better than most. This type of gentle rolling terrain is ideal for practicing for steeper ups and downs.
- Several highways are not plowed in winter. The Alpine Scenic Loop, American Fork Canyon above Tipple Fork Reservoir, upper Emigration Canyon, upper City Creek Canyon, the Skyline Trail above Bountiful, the Guardsman's Pass road between Brighton and Park City, and many miles of roads in the Park City/Midway area are very suitable for ski touring. Snowmobiles can be a hazard, but the terrain is good.
- The Park City/Snyderville region is ideal for beginner tours, but most of the land is privately owned and heavy usage is often discouraged. One exception is Thaynes Canyon, which is part of the Park City Resort. In the past, the owners have allowed cross country skiers to hike up the road. The

Figure 3-1—This young tourer took his first faltering steps on skis in a Salt Lake City cemetary. As you can see, he quickly developed championship form.

lower part of Thaynes, starting near the Silver King Mine Train entrance, is good for the novice who is ready to get away from the golf course.

BEGINNING SKI TOURS

The tours described in this chapter are listed roughly in order of increasing difficulty. Some of the easier ones are simply the lower parts of the canyons which are described in later chapters as more advanced outings. A beginner can tour up a canyon until the terrain gets too steep to enjoy, and then turn around and ski back down. Be aware that the difficulty of a ski tour is not easy to define. It depends to a large extent upon the condition of the snow, which can change very quickly due to snowfall, wind and temperature. The weather, the physical condition of the tourer, the particular route chosen, and equipment are also

Figure 3-2—Slowing down on a hard track can cause great concern for the beginning tourer. If there is no room to ski into deep snow beside the track, you can use your poles as a brake. Don't push too hard with tonkin poles, though, or you'll have the wrong kind of break!

important. For the skiers using cross-country equipment, correct technique and proper wax make all the difference in the world.

It is advisable for a novice to try some of the first tours described in this chapter before undertaking the latter ones. The more difficult outings require more endurance and/or better downhill technique. The beginning ski tourer should master the kick-turn early. This will assure a safe descent over almost any terrain via the "survival method" of traversing across the slope, kick-turning, traversing back, etc. An enthusiastic learner will not long be able to resist the exhilaration of zooming through the powder with snow spraying in all directions.

Beginners who have trouble slowing down on trails that are well packed and fast might consider a couple of suggestions for a more controlled descent. When the snow beside the trail is soft, skiing with one ski in the powder and one in the track will slow you down. Both skis in the deep snow works even better. It is advisable to go into powder snow gradually to avoid taking a nose dive! Another alternative is to drag your ski poles on the side or between your legs; pushing down harder slows you down even more. (This is not recommended for wooden poles except in cases of extreme panic.)

Lower Millcreek Canyon

The Millcreek highway is plowed to the Forest Service Guard Station, about 0.5 mile beyond Log Haven Restaurant, with room for parking and turning around at the end. The canyon is open to snowmobiles, but there are usually very few because the road is too narrow to turn a trailer around. Tourers and walkers have increasingly found this to be a convenient spot for leisurely outings. It is the closest location to Salt Lake City which has consistent snow and good beginning terrain.

The road rises very gradually for about 4.5 miles, and the Millcreek drainage continues for another three miles beyond that. About 3.1 miles up from the parking area there is an open spring on the right that offers the thirsty tourer a refreshing drink any time of year. Aside from an occasional cabin, upper Millcreek Canyon in winter has a most primitive atmosphere. Little vestige remains of a once booming area which boasted twenty sawmills cutting lumber for the pioneers in the valley.

Chapter 4 is devoted to the ski tours in the side canyons on the south slopes of Millcreek.

Silver Lake/Redman Campground

One of the nicest areas for a beginner to practice his touring technique is the flat terrain around Silver Lake at Brighton. The lake is in the large meadow across from the village store. It is usually frozen over by the time the snow is good, but you should be careful early in the season. Both north and south of the lake are wooded areas with roads winding through the trees. The brightly painted cabins make it look like a little Switzerland with snowy peaks rising in the background. There is plenty of room to park on the right side of the highway across from the Brighton Store.

Another relatively flat location for beginning tourers is Redman Campground, just above the Solitude ski area. This is one place where a skier can often find a good track already packed out. Roads and trails wander through the firs and aspens all the way down to Solitude and up toward Brighton. Big Cottonwood Creek can be difficult to cross, even in the middle of the winter, but there are several bridges over it in the campground. The Utah Highway Department has been kind enough to plow a parking area here to cater to the many tourers who enjoy the gentle terrain and relative seclusion of the campground.

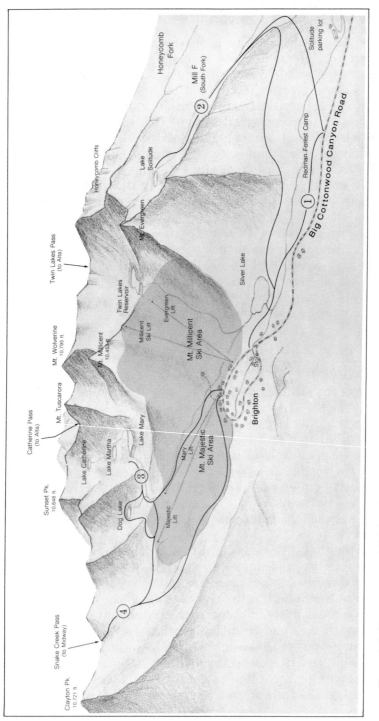

Figure 3-3—The area around Brighton is particularly suitable for beginning ski tourers. The numbered routes are described in this chapter. 1. Silver Lake/Redman Campground. 2. Lake Solitude. 3. Brighton Lakes. 4. Snake Creek Pass.

Figure 3-4—A good starting tour is between Redman Campground just above Solitude, and Silver Lake at Brighton. The terrain is quite gentle and the sounds of cars on the road can help you keep your bearings.

When you're ready to try a tour of a mile or so with a bit of uphill and/or downhill, the trip from Redman Campground to Silver Lake or vice versa is a good one. It is best to wait until three or four feet of snow is on the ground since there is no trail to follow. The best landmarks are on the lower end, so the route is easier to find from Redman to Brighton. (See the photo in Fig. 3-4.) A telephone line and a power line run parallel to the highway near the campground. Simply follow the phone line as it rises gradually through a wide swath cut in the trees. About 0.5 mile from the parking area, a second telephone line crosses the first at right angles. Turn right there and traverse up the hill through the fir trees and summer homes. Keep bearing left and climbing at a comfortable rate. When the terrain levels off at the top, head for the Brighton ski lifts, and Silver Lake will soon appear.

When starting at Brighton, proceed toward Silver Lake from the store. After passing the first row of trees, bear right

71

Figure 3-5—The road from Solitude to the Alta Mine in lower Silver Fork is a delightful beginner tour with very little elevation change. This area is shown in the map of the south side of Big Cottonwood (Figure 6-8).

and follow the roadway to the north through the summer home area. Turn right again beyond the first group of houses and traverse gradually downhill, taking as steep a line as is comfortable. The route passes through an area of large fir trees, then another group of homes. If you take a steep enough traverse, you will encounter the phone line that goes straight to Redman Campground.

Lower Silver Fork

Silver Fork is one of several Wasatch canyons that have very challenging terrain at the top, but allow delightful beginner tours when approached from the bottom. The best starting point is the lower parking lot of the Solitude ski area. A road begins at the far end of the parking lot and goes around to the right of the lower end of the ski lift. (Don't take the road that goes up through the trees near the end of the parking lot.) After passing the lift, follow the road generally to the north where it enters the evergreens. This is the access for some of the summer homes in Silver Fork and is usually well packed by snowmobiles. It is about a mile to the cabin area. The trail turns up the canyon just beyond the large building on the left that overlooks the highway. It's hard to believe that 100 years ago one could look down on the town of Silver Springs from this spot. The thriving mining community had a hotel, a post office, 2 stores, a smelter, several houses, and numerous homes.

A few hundred yards up the fork, the trail crosses the stream and stays on the right side of the drainage for the rest of the tour. The terrain gets somewhat steeper a mile or so up the canyon, so beginners will want to stop there. Just across the stream from that point are the tunnels of the old Alta mine, which was one of several very rich silver lodes in the canyon. About the only activities in the area today are hiking and touring, with a bit of snowmobiling by residents of the nearby cabins.

Mill F East Fork

Mill F is the uppermost of the "mill" forks in Big Cottonwood Canyon. These were named for the series of seven sawmills set up by the Mormon settlers in the 1850's and 1860's to provide lumber for their extensive building program. Output of just three mills in the vicinity of Mill F and Brighton produced more than 1,000,000 board feet annually for many years.

The east fork of Mill F begins across the highway from the Solitude ski area, and its two branches lead to Scott's Pass and Guardsman's Pass. The best access route starts just across from the entrance to the upper Solitude parking lot. Usually you can find room to park on either side of the highway during the daytime.

The Mill F access road goes north from the highway through some aspens past a group of summer homes and then into an open area. The canyon goes up to the right at this point. The road provides a good touring route along the left side of the drainage almost all the way to Scott's Pass, which is about 2.5 miles and 1500 vertical feet from the highway. One of the more noteworth landmarks of the tour is a handsomely decorated outhouse beside the trail with aspens painted on all sides. It looks quite inviting, but, alas, it is kept locked!

Another half mile beyond this, a power line comes in from the right and follows the road to where the terrain gets steep just below the pass. The open tunnel on the left is the old Iowa-

Figure 3-6—Mill F North Fork starts across from Solitude and ends at the Park City ridge. Its two branches lead to Scotts and Guardsmans passes. Fig. 6-15 is a map of the area.

Copper Mine. (Remember that some of these tunnels are extremely hazardous, so exploring is not recommended.)

The only difficult part of the tour is the last quarter mile from the end of the power line to the pass. It requires considerable traversing and kick-turning, but the view of Park City and the Uinta Mountains beyond is outstanding. Scott's Pass is at the head of Thaynes Canyon, which has some excellent touring terrain down to the Park City ski area.

The second branch of Mill F East Fork leads to Guardsman's Pass. An easy way to get into this drainage is to turn right through the open area just beyond the decorated outhouse. The road to the pass is soon encountered. The terrain is just as good and the view at the top is equally spectacular. Unfortunately, the snowmobiles have better access to this branch. It might be better to save it for a midweek outing.

Figure 3-7—Big and Little Cottonwood Canyons are in the Salt Lake County watershed, so conscientious tourers should avoid leaving anything in the snow that they would not want in their drinking water the next spring.

Lake Solitude

You say you want to get away from the "sights and sounds of civilization"? This is the place! Mill F South Fork is the home of aptly named Lake Solitude, which is nestled in a bowl surrounded on three sides by extremely steep slopes. The tour can be done from Brighton or from the Redman Campground. It is 0.5 mile longer from Brighton, but the route is easier, with 300 instead of 600 feet of elevation change. Both are marked on the photo in Fig. 3-8.

The first alternative is to park across from the store at Brighton and head for Silver Lake. Early in the season it is best to go to the right around the lake. When all signs of water seeping up through the snow are gone, it is usually safe to cut across. When crossing the lake, head for the two clumps of large fir trees at the base of the steep ridge that comes down north of the ski lifts. The trail goes through the trees and along the level ground for about 100 yards. It then passes to the left of a lone fir tree and begins a gradual traverse up through some aspens (this section is well marked by names carved in the trees) and

Figure 3-8 — Lake Solitude is most easily reached from Brighton. With a bit more climbing, the tour can be done from Redman Campground. The steep slopes around the lake are extremely hazardous and should be avoided.

later through another area of large fir trees. About a mile from Brighton the trail turns sharply to the left and climbs gradually along the left side of the Mill F South Fork drainage. Just below Lake Solitude there is a steep open slope on the left that should be avoided. Bear right into the bottom of the canyon at this point, and go up across the meadow to the road on the other side that leads to the lake.

The other alternative is to start at Redman Campground. Cross the creek and go to the right toward the Solitude ski area. The first 300 feet of elevation must be gained by traversing back and forth across or near the first ski trails. Mill F South bears to the left away from the ski area and climbs gradually for another half mile to Lake Solitude. The road along the right side of the drainage is a good route to follow.

The Mill F road continues along the right side of the lake to the Solitude Mine tunnel on the far side. This is an entrance to one of the most extensive systems of tunnels in the Wasatch. It is part of the Michigan-Utah mine in Grizzly Gulch just above

76

Figure 3-9—Albion Basin is a delightful place in any season. Powder snow in winter, sun in spring, flowers in summer and fall make it a favorite of Salt Lake skiers and hikers.

Alta. Anyone venturing away from the lake should be aware that the slopes around it are extremely prone to avalanche. In fact, several people were killed in this canyon in the years when mining flourished. It is best to stay completely away from any steep areas unless the snow is absolutely stable.

Albion Basin

Despite the proximity of the Alta ski area, Albion Basin is one of the most pleasant touring spots in the Wasatch, especially on a sunny afternoon in March when spring fever has taken its first bite. The basin itself is a large flat area with huge fir trees scattered about and lots of delightful spots to enjoy a picnic. Several people have cabins in the area, so you may see a snow cat or two, but extensive development of Albion Basin has thus far been prohibited. Let's hope the condominium builders don't get their way in this beautiful spot. The town of Alta had as many as 8,000 residents in the old mining days, but it's much more pleasant today.

Access to Albion Basin is via a Forest Service road that is the continuation of the Little Cottonwood highway. Simply stay to the left through Alta and beyond all the ski lifts and lodge parking areas. There is usually plenty of parking at the end of the plowed road. The tour route rises gradually with one large switchback and eventually goes under one of the ski lifts and into Albion Basin. There is some congestion at the top with skiers coming off the lifts, but that is quickly left behind.

It should be mentioned that if time is too short or you don't feel ambitious enough to hike the 1.5 miles and 600 vertical feet into Albion Basin, single ride passes for the ski lift are available.

The lower part of Albion Basin is ideal for anyone who enjoys flat terrain. The upper section has some excellent slopes for aspiring intermediate skiers. Tourers climbing into the basin must be particularly aware of avalanche hazard on the open slopes under Devil's Castle on the right, and the chutes under Point Supreme on the left. (Fig. 3-9 is an aerial photo of the area.)

Mill D North Fork (Dog Lake/Desolation Lake)

Beginning skiers will find the last three tours in this chapter a little more difficult than the others. They all have sections that can be quite challenging to someone who is not yet able to maneuver between the trees. This can be less of a problem in deep powder, which slows a skier down, so those who can't turn would be wise to save these tours for the right snow conditions. Snowshoers will not find this to be a problem.

The lakes in Mill D North Fork are both small muddy puddles in the summer, often with motorcycles buzzing around like flies on carrion. This area is much more pleasant in the winter months, although snowmobiles do sometimes stray into the canyon. The trail up Mill D starts just below and across the highway from the Spruces Campground. The easiest way into the fork is the summer home access road that traverses up the east side from the highway. Just beyond the last cabin on the left, a trail goes through the aspens toward the bottom of the drainage and stays near the stream all the way to the lakes. About 2.0 miles from the road, the canyon branches left to Dog Lake and right to Desolation Lake. The elevation gain to this point is only 850 feet, so the first part of the tour is suitable for any beginner; beyond the branch point it gets more challenging.

DOG LAKE. The shorter alternative is Dog Lake, about 0.8 mile and 550 vertical feet farther. Part of the trail is quite

Figure 3-10—Dog Lake is at the top of the west branch of Mill D North Fork. Two descent routes are shown in the photo, along with access points for Millcreek Canyon tours. Figure 6-15 is a map of this area.

narrow and steep, but there is a better route down for the faint-hearted. Simply keep to the left when you get to the lake and go over the rise into the drainage that parallels the one you came up. They merge just above the Desolation Lake turn-off. The open areas in the firs on the right as you go down can provide some good practice terrain for powder skiing if avalanche conditions permit.

DESOLATION LAKE. Desolation Lake is about 2.0 miles and 1100 vertical feet from the branch point. Most of the trail is in flat open meadows, but some parts are a bit steeper. It starts out with a climb through an aspen forest, then bears to the right down into the bottom of the drainage. Follow the open meadows, keeping to the left in the wooded areas, all the way to the lake. There is a small lake on the right below Desolation Lake, but the trail continues along the left side of the canyon. There are many extremely hazardous slopes along the south side of upper Mill D which should always be given a wide berth. (Fig. 3-11.)

79

Figure 3-11—Desolation Lake is tucked into a bowl at the end of the east branch of Mill D North Fork. This canyon provides access to upper Millcreek Canyon, Beartrap Fork and terrain south of the Park West ski area.

Brighton Lakes (Dog Lake/Lake Mary)

Yes, Virginia, there really are two Dog Lakes. This one is about 0.4 mile west of the top of the Majestic lift at Brighton, and Lake Mary is another 0.2 mile beyond (Figure 3-12). As with the Albion Basin tour, the lift can be used to avoid most of the climb, but it saves only about a mile and 600 vertical feet. The

Figure 3-12—The Brighton Lakes area has some spectacular scenery for the beginning tourer who has progressed far enough to be able to handle a bit of downhill skiing.

best route for hiking up the mountain is in the woods to the right of the Mary lift. Steep slopes on the right eventually force you out onto a ski trail, but the traffic is not usually very heavy on the edge. It is somewhat disconcerting to watch the flailing masses of "yoyo" skiers hurtling out of control in your direction, but when you're in their territory, you can only hope for the best.

DOG LAKE.   A good approach to Dog Lake is from the top of the Majestic lift, where you bear right and go through an opening in the trees into a large meadow. Bear right again and head for the upper corner of this meadow, where a road leads through an evergreen forest to Dog Lake. This road was originally built to service the Big Cottonwood mine, which is on the left just before the lake. There are some very steep avalanche slopes above the mine, so when conditions are at all unstable, tourers should not venture away from the road in that direction. Dog Lake is surrounded on three sides by open areas that have good terrain for those wishing to practice their downhill technique.

The Dog Lake loop is completed by continuing on the road from the mine along the left side of the lake. At the point where the terrain drops off quite steeply, the Brighton Lakes Trail traverses to the right and down to the ski area. Getting back to the parking lot from here is the reason this tour is listed so late in the chapter. You can either work your way down through the trees on the left where you came up, or you can brave the packed slopes and dodge the hot-doggers. Some turning ability will be required either way. Don't hesitate to use the traverse and kick-turn technique, or you could take off your skis and walk!

LAKE MARY.   Lake Mary is about 200 vertical feet above Dog Lake, and is most easily reached via the Brighton Lakes Trail just mentioned. It intersects the ski area just above the top of the Mary Lift where the ski trail makes a sharp left turn. Go right at this point and traverse through the firs up to the flat area that overlooks the village of Brighton. From there just follow the drainage that winds up to the Lake Mary dam. A couple of traverses will get you one of the most spectacular views in the Wasatch. Mt. Tuscarora, Wolverine, and Millicent provide an impressive backdrop for the lake.

Snake Creek Pass

The last tour in this chapter is also in the Brighton area. Snake Creek Pass is southwest of Clayton Peak and overlooks Heber Valley and the Uintas beyond. It is reputed to be one of the finest spots in Utah from which to view a sunrise, but only the hard core have experienced this phenomenon. The total climb from the parking lot to the pass is about 1.5 miles and 1,200 vertical feet, but once again you can eliminate half of that with a single ride ticket for the Majestic lift.

The two alternatives for the Snake Creek Pass tour are shown in Figure 3-13. One is from the top of the Majestic lift.

Figure 3-13—Snake Creek Pass above Brighton overlooks Heber and the Uinta Mountains to the east. Snake Creek, which runs from the pass down to Wasatch State Park in Midway, is a good intermediate tour, but the car shuttle is prohibitively long.

(See the previous tour description for details of how to get there.) Bear right through the opening in the trees into the meadow, but instead of going farther right toward Dog Lake, go left and follow the series of open areas that lead up toward the pass. The last 200 feet of elevation are steeper and more wooded, so some traversing back and forth through the firs is necessary.

The second alternative is more   pleasant because it is more secluded. It is particularly advantageous coming down, since it avoids the packed slopes. The route from the parking lot is in the trees to the left of the Majestic lift. Gradually work your way into the bottom of the drainage that parallels the lift and follow it all the way to Snake Creek Pass. A few powder hounds may be encountered, but the traffic is much lighter this way. □

4 MILLCREEK CANYON

Millcreek is one of the least known but most accessible ski touring areas in the Wasatch Mountains. It has long been a favorite for fishermen, hikers, picnickers, and bikers in the summer, but winter use has become popular only in the past couple of years since the highway department has made an attempt to block off motor traffic. Growing numbers of skiers, snowshoers, and even hikers are enjoying the tree-lined, snow-covered road above the Forest Service Guard Station. This road was described in Chapter 3 as one of the better places for beginning cross country skiers.

The area that is not so well known is the terrain far above the highway near the ridge that separates Millcreek and Big Cottonwood Canyons. Some of the high bowls provide excellent opportunities for the intermediate or advanced ski tourer who enjoys a run in the powder. One difficulty with Millcreek tours is that they are best done from Big Cottonwood Canyon. A car shuttle is involved unless you are prepared to hike several miles along the road then up a side canyon to the ridge. A considerable elevation and distance advantage is gained by using Mill D North Fork or Butler Fork as an approach.

Millcreek is one of the most heavily wooded Wasatch canyons. As its name implies, this fact was noted by the early

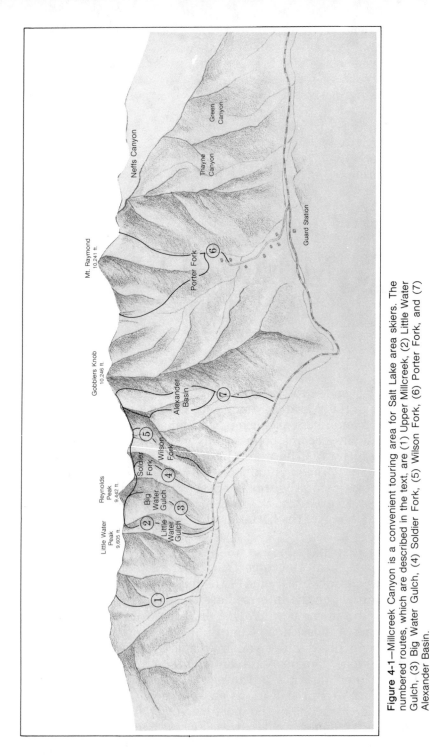

Figure 4-1—Millcreek Canyon is a convenient touring area for Salt Lake area skiers. The numbered routes, which are described in the text, are (1) Upper Millcreek, (2) Little Water Gulch, (3) Big Water Gulch, (4) Soldier Fork, (5) Wilson Fork, (6) Porter Fork, and (7) Alexander Basin.

pioneers, who set up many sawmills there to help provide for the needs of their growing community. Most of the side canyons, in fact, were named for the men who operated these mills. The heavy vegetation has benefits as well as disadvantages for a skier. The upper bowls are generally less avalanche-prone than their counterparts in other canyons (with some very notable exceptions!) Early in the season, however, when snow cover is light, the lower sections of most Millcreek forks are too brushy for enjoyable skiing.

Another potential problem in Millcreek Canyon is the relatively low elevation of much of the touring terrain. Prevailing snow conditions are very critical to the enjoyment of a tour. Late in the winter when temperatures begin to rise, the snow is heavier than that in the Brighton and Alta areas.

The tours described in this chapter are all of intermediate difficulty, with the exception of Alexander Basin, which is in a class by itself. They are listed in geographic order starting at the upper end of the canyon. This is generally in order of increasing challenge of the descent. The lower forks have more trees and brush to dodge, lower quality and quantity of snow, and steeper sections near the highway. Fig. 4-1 is a map of the south side of the canyon showing all the tours that are described in this chapter.

INTERMEDIATE TOURS

Most of the terrain in Millcreek Canyon is suitable for an intermediate skier. Six such tours are described in the following sections.

Upper Millcreek

The easiest of the Millcreek tours is a run down the bottom of the drainage from the top end of the canyon. It is ranked intermediate rather than beginner only because of its length. Regardless of the starting point, the climb is more than 3.5 miles and at least 2300 vertical feet. Three routes are described here for the hike to the top, each starting from a different canyon: Millcreek, Mill D North in Big Cottonwood, and Red Pine near the Park West ski area.

The run down Millcreek is the same for all. Simply ski through the aspens at the top and follow the stream bed to the

Figure 4-2—Upper Millcreek Canyon can be approached from the Park West ski area, Big Cottonwood, or Lower Mill-creek. The plowed highway ends about eight miles from the top of the canyon.

end of the highway, a distance of 3.4 miles. Then follow the road for another 4.6 miles to where the snowplow stops. This provides a total of 3600 feet of elevation change. The terrain is quite gentle and should provide little difficulty even for a novice skier, but the tour requires good physical condition, particularly if the snow is deep. Note in Fig. 4-2 that it is possible to drop into upper Millcreek from the south ridge of the canyon. Caution is urged on these slopes due to avalanche hazard.

UPPER MILLCREEK FROM LOWER MILLCREEK.   The tour along the canyon bottom into the upper reaches of Millcreek was described in Chapter 3. (The route is the reverse of the descent just described.) It is a beautiful area for the skier who enjoys a long, relatively flat hike. There is usually very little traffic beyond the first two miles, although an occasional skier or snowmobile makes it beyond the end of the highway. You can climb a total of 8.0 miles to the Park City ridge for a view of the Uintas to the east.

UPPER MILLCREEK FROM BIG COTTONWOOD CANYON.   The head of Millcreek Canyon can be reached most easily from Mill D North Fork in Big Cottonwood. A climb of only 2300 feet over 3.7 miles is required. The route follows the Desolation Lake trail described in Chapter 3 (Fig. 3-11). After climbing through the aspens above the intersection with the Dog Lake trail, bear left and follow the drainage just north of the one leading to Desolation Lake. Some of the slopes along the right side of this drainage are particularly good for powder skiing, so a side trip may be in order. At the top of this canyon is a minor peak which is common to the Big Cottonwood, Millcreek, and Park City areas. A short traverse along the Park City ridge takes you to a good spot to start a run down through the aspens.

UPPER MILLCREEK FROM PARK WEST. The east ridge at the top of Millcreek borders the Park West ski area between Murdock Peak and Red Pine Canyon. The 2600 foot ascent from the parking lot can be done via chair lift, by hiking up a downhill ski trail, or by the more scenic route in Red Pine Canyon just south of the developed ski area. Regardless of which route is chosen, you should check with the Ski Patrol or the Ski Touring School before attempting this climb. They will be aware of avalanche conditions at the higher elevations.

Little Water Gulch / Little Water Peak

The first peak on the Millcreek/Big Cottonwood ridge is Little Water, which lies at the head of the gulch with the same name. The peak is about a mile from the end of the canyon, and the gulch intersects the Millcreek stream just above the end of the highway.

The area got its name from the springs that originate there, contributing to an abundant year-round flow of water in Millcreek Canyon. The quantity of water was, in fact, one reason for the large number of sawmills that once existed there. The water is now used primarily for irrigation in the valley, although at one time there was a plan to divert much of Millcreek's water to Lambs Canyon via an aqueduct under the mountains. This was proposed as a part of the controversial Little Dell project in Parleys Canyon.

Little Water Peak can be reached from Park West or from the Millcreek highway, but the most direct approach is from Mill D North Fork in Big Cottonwood. Simply climb to Dog Lake (2.8 miles with 1400 feet of elevation gain) and follow the ridge east for another 0.9 miles to the peak. See Chapter 3 and Fig. 3-10 for details. The top is only 9422 feet, so total climb involves about 2100 vertical feet.

Figure 4-3—The Water Gulches are very accessible from Mill D North Fork in Big Cottonwood. They intersect the main canyon near the end of the highway.

The two most common descent routes are shown in Fig. 4-3. First is Little Water Gulch. The run down to the Millcreek stream is very straightforward. There may be some brush early in the season, but it should present no problem for mid-winter tours. The snow is often best on the west side of the gulch. Total descent to the end of the highway is 1.8 miles and 1600 vertical feet.

The second descent route from Little Water Peak is in the drainage just east of Little Water Gulch. The steep open bowl northeast of the summit should always be avoided. It usually has a large cornice at the top, and avalanches are common. A less hazardous alternative is along the ridge north from the peak and then down through the trees as shown in the photo. The remainder of the tour is a relatively gentle descent to the Millcreek stream and then a 4.8 mile run to your car.

Big Water Gulch

The most accessible of the Millcreek side canyons is Big Water Gulch. Dog Lake lies near its head, so the approach from Big Cottonwood is only a 1400 foot climb. The bottom of the gulch is at the end of the Millcreek highway. This area is motor-cycle heaven in the summer months, so winter is the best time to enjoy it.

Big Water almost became part of "Sugarbush West", a downhill skiing facility proposed for the end of the Millcreek Canyon road. A few years ago, a square mile of land was purchased by the individual who owned the Sugarbush Ski Area in Vermont. He applied for permits to develop a large part of upper Millcreek into a huge ski/condominium complex. This would have involved widening the road and destroying parts of the stream bed. Fortunately, the Forest Service and Salt Lake County agreed that the idea wasn't a good one, and fishermen, picnickers, and ski tourers continue to enjoy this part of the canyon.

To get to the top of Big Water Gulch, follow Mill D North Fork to Dog Lake (Chapter 3, Fig. 3-10). The west side of the gulch often has the best snow, so you can traverse northwest-ward from Dog Lake along the north side of Reynolds Peak, as shown in Fig. 4-3. There is a trail through the fir trees that makes this an easy traverse. A short hike along the ridge, over a small shoulder, takes you to a good place to start the descent. Distance from the Big Cottonwood highway is 3.2 miles.

The route down is very simple. It follows the drainage for 1.4 miles and 1200 vertical feet to the highway, and then winds its way another 4.6 miles to the point where the plows stop.

Soldier Fork

The canyon west of the Water Gulches is Soldier Fork. It is somewhat steeper than its easterly neighbors, with some avalanche hazard in the upper bowl, but the skiing can be delightful in the aspens and firs when there is enough snow to cover the undergrowth. The bottom end of Soldier is just below the end of the Millcreek highway.

An easy touring route into the top of Soldier Fork is simply a continuation of that into Big Water Gulch. From Dog Lake (see Chapter 3) traverse along the north side of Reynolds Peak to the head of Butler Fork. Follow the ridge between Millcreek and Big Cottonwood (Fig. 4-4) beyond the top of Big Water to the point that you choose as a starting place for the run down to the highway. The central part of the upper bowl is the most protected from avalanche hazard, with groups of trees going all

Figure 4-4—The Millcreek/Big Cottonwood ridge between Dog Lake and Gobblers Knob provides access to Big Water Gulch, Soldier Fork, Wilson Fork, and Alexander Basin.

the way to the top. The west side of the canyon is more open and steep (Fig. 4-5).

An alternative approach to Soldier Fork is via Butler, which is described in Chapter 6. This is slightly shorter, but it has more elevation to gain. The hike from the bottom of Mill D North to the top of Soldier via Dog Lake is 3.3 miles with 1600 feet of vertical. The Butler Fork route is 2.1 miles and 1900 vertical feet.

The run down Soldier Fork to the Millcreek stream is only 1300 vertical feet over 1.1 miles, with an additional 4.5 miles to the end of the plowed highway.

Wilson Fork

The canyons that empty into Millcreek get longer, steeper, and narrower as you go westward toward Gobblers Knob. The

Figure 4-5—Soldier Fork and Wilson Fork are somewhat more challenging than the tours farther up Millcreek, but both have good intermediate terrain. Note that the west sides of the canyons are steeper and more susceptible to avalanches.

northeast-facing headwall at the top of Wilson Fork should be avoided in all but the most stable snow conditions. The lower part of the canyon has a gully that can be challenging to the intermediate skier, particularly if several people have already made tracks in the snow. As Fig. 4-5 illustrates, the problem areas can be avoided if a good route is chosen.

The alternatives for climbing to the top of Wilson are the same as those just mentioned for Soldier. The most common is to hike up Mill D North Fork to Dog Lake, as described in the preceding chapter. From the lake, a traverse around the north side of Reynolds Peak and then a 1.8 mile climb along the Millcreek ridge takes you to the highest point of Wilson Fork (Fig. 4-4). The total climb is 2600 feet over 4.7 miles. Another possibility is to tour up Butler Fork to the end and then follow the ridge to the peak at the top of Wilson. This is 3.5 miles with an elevation gain of 2900 feet.

After enjoying the view and some lunch, the cautious skier

will undoubtedly want to retrace his climbing route down to the low point in the center of Wilson's upper bowl. The trees offer good protection for a descent at this point. Another safe way off the peak is to follow the ridge that goes in a northerly direction between Wilson Fork and Alexander Basin. About 1000 vertical feet down the ridge, you can safely bear right into the Wilson drainage.

The narrow gully in the lower part of the fork is sheltered from wind and sun, so it can be a good place for powder snow. If it has been too heavily skied, however, you may prefer to stay in the aspens on the west side of the canyon. The trees are far enough apart to be enjoyable for a reasonably competent skier. The total downhill run from the top of Wilson Fork to the highway is 1.8 miles with 2500 feet of vertical. Another 4.2 miles gets you to the car.

Porter Fork/Gobblers Knob

Porter Fork is the largest of the Millcreek side canyons. At least five of its branches are good for skiing, with possibilities for tours involving Big Cottonwood or Neffs Canyon. The fork was named after Chauncey Porter who set up the first sawmill in Millcreek Canyon. It has also been the home of several mines that stayed active for many years; in fact, at least one of them is still being worked. Lower Porter is presently a summer cottage area with a paved road that winds 1.3 miles up from the Millcreek highway.

The most famous miner in Porter was Indian Pete, a drifter who settled in the upper reaches of the canyon in the 1880's to try to make his fortune. He was unsuccessful and met an untimely end in an avalanche in the winter of 1889. The Indian Pete Mining and Milling Company was formed a few years later, and his name was carried on in Millcreek history.

The four tours described in this section go to the pass west of Mount Raymond (the "standard" tour), the saddle between Mount Raymond and Gobblers Knob (usually approached from Big Cottonwood), Neffs Canyon ridge, and Gobblers Knob. These are intended to be in order of increasing difficulty, but snow conditions and route selection make a tremendous difference in the narrow brushy terrain in Millcreek. Skiing at such a low elevation is an uncertain proposition.

STANDARD PORTER FORK TOUR. The Porter Fork road intersects the Millcreek highway about 0.2 miles above Log

Figure 4-6—The largest Millcreek side canyon is Porter Fork. Some of the tours that are described involve Alexander Basin, Gobblers Knob, Big Cottonwood, and Neffs. Mount Raymond is also at the head of Porter, but it is too steep and rocky for good skiing.

95

Haven Restaurant. Ski tours from the bottom of the fork start along the road through the cabin area. Above the summer homes are some switchbacks followed by more gentle terrain. The road continues through an aspen forest and into an open area below a steep bowl. Straight ahead is a picturesque rock formation with a large cave high above the trail. To get to the pass west of Mount Raymond, you should bear left at this point and continue climbing along the drainage to the east of the cave rock. This leads to the pass overlooking Big Cottonwood and other areas to the south. Total climb from the highway is 3400 vertical feet over 3.5 miles.

Options for the descent are somewhat limited. The most obvious is to retrace the climbing route back to Millcreek. An alternative is to ski the slopes on the west side of the fork down to the cave rock. Care must be taken to avoid avalanche paths that come down through the trees in this area (Fig. 4-6). Lower Porter Fork is much too heavily wooded to allow any deviation from the road.

PORTER FORK FROM BIG COTTONWOOD. The saddle between Mount Raymond and Gobblers Knob is most easily reached from Butler Fork in Big Cottonwood Canyon. The approach, which is described in detail in Chapter 6, is a climb up the west branch of Butler and a traverse across the upper part of Mill A Basin to the pass. This is 3.0 miles with a 2200 foot elevation gain.

In order to avoid a car shuttle, the pass can be reached from the bottom of Porter Fork. Simply follow the road up through the cabins and then the switchbacks. When the terrain levels off, bear left off the road through the aspens and up to the pass. This area can be confusing because the trees are too thick to allow a view of either Gobblers or Raymond until you have climbed quite a ways. Be careful to avoid the avalanche paths noted in Fig. 4-6.

The descent from the saddle is along the route just described. Follow the drainage almost to the Porter Fork road. When the gully becomes too narrow and steep, traverse left to the road and follow it down through the switchbacks and cabin area. The descent is 3.6 miles with 3400 feet of elevation change.

NEFFS CANYON FROM PORTER FORK. A short section of the west ridge of Porter is common to Neffs. (See Fig. 4-6.) The terrain below this ridge is much too steep to be a safe climb in winter. A better approach to Neffs is along the ridge as shown in the photo. From the end of the cabin area in Porter, turn right and climb the ridge that goes west from the road. After about 300 feet of elevation have been gained, bear right and traverse into an open side canyon. The ridge on the north side of that canyon is a good climbing route all the way to the top of Neffs. Total climb from the Millcreek highway is 3.5 miles with a gain of 3800 vertical feet.

The remainder of this tour is described in the next chapter.

GOBBLERS KNOB.   The north slope of this peak is the wide expanse of white that is visible from Salt Lake in the winter. Formerly known as Porter Peak, this 10,246 foot summit is called Gobblers Knob* on the topographical maps. It is the highest point in the Big Cottonwood/Millcreek ridge. Surprisingly, the rocks at the summit were once on the floor of an ancient sea. Fossils are in abundance for the summer visitor to observe.

The peak should be approached along one of the ridges that lead to the top. The safest route is from the saddle between Gobblers and Raymond, which is about 900 feet below the summit. Total climb is 4.0 miles with 3100 feet of elevation gain from Big Cottonwood via Butler Fork, or 4.5 miles and 4300 feet via Porter.

Gobblers looks inviting to the powder lover, but the area can be extremely hazardous unless avalanche conditions are absolutely stable. Also, there is little protection from the wind, so the snow is often not as good as it appears from the valley. The descent route for the cautious tourer is back down the ridge to the saddle. Another possibility is the ridge to the north between Porter and Alexander Basin. You can ski about 1000 vertical feet down the ridge into safe terrain, then traverse left to the Porter Fork drainage. You can also turn right at that point and find a good entry into Alexander Basin.

ADVANCED TOURS

The only Millcreek fork that has been classified as advanced is Alexander Basin. It is steeper at both top and bottom than any

---

*Gobblers Knob may have received its unusual name from miners in the area who tried to supplement their meager earnings by raising turkeys, an undertaking that was no more successful than their diggings. It is also possible that the peak was named for a mayor of Salt Lake City who reportedly climbed to one of the nearby mines and scolded the residents for allowing their canine companions to roam in the watershed, and soon thereafter mounted a campaign to encourage commercial development in the same watershed.

other, there is considerably more avalanche hazard as Fig. 4-7 shows, and a longer climb is required to get to the top.

Alexander Basin

Alexander Basin is another of the Millcreek side canyons named after a man who cut and hauled timber in the area. Alva Alexander and his sons ran a sawmill there in the nineteenth century. Judging from the number and size of the stumps visible in summer, the basin must have been one of the most heavily logged canyons in Millcreek.

There is a legend associated with one of the mills at Alexander Flat. The owner reportedly had a problem with tools disappearing. He was not successful in discovering how they were being removed, and soon he didn't have enough tools to be able to continue operation. In desperation, he called in Brigham Young for advice. The Mormon leader suggested that the owner may have offended the spirits of people who had lived there previously by building the mill on sacred ground. The mill was moved and the problem never again occurred.[†]

Three tours will be described for Alexander Basin. In order of increasing difficulty, they are lower Alexander from Porter, the east branch of the basin, and upper Alexander. The last is so steep and dangerous that it should be attempted only by an expert skier who is either fearless or foolhardy (or both, since the former implies the latter). The first two tours are extremely challenging but relatively safe.

LOWER ALEXANDER BASIN FROM PORTER FORK. The easiest route into the basin is over the ridge from the west and into the lower part of the cirque as shown in Fig. 4-7. Most of

---

[†] The sage advice of Brigham Young has in many cases proven to be relevant to modern day situations. For example, he was once asked about what constitutes health, wealth, joy, and peace. "In the first place," he stated, "good pure air is the greatest sustainer of animal life. Other elements of life we can dispense with for a time.... You can live without water or food longer than you can without air, and water is more important than meat or bread." Brigham Young was certainly Utah's first—and possibly our only—leader with a genuine concern for long range planning and preservation of the environment. (Photo courtesy of Utah State Historical Society.)

Figure 4-7—The most hazardous area in Millcreek Canyon is upper Alexander Basin. The east branch is much safer, as is the route into the lower part of the basin from Porter Fork.

the hazardous areas can be avoided by carefully selecting the point of descent from the ridge.

The climb was partially described in the Porter Fork section. Simply hike up the road through the cabin area and the switchbacks above. When the road flattens out, bear left and follow the drainage toward the saddle between Mount Raymond and Gobblers Knob. Traverse left in the wooded area below the open slopes that extend to the summit of Gobblers. This traverse intersects the ridge that separates Porter and Alexander (Fig. 4-6). The ascent is 4.1 miles with 3300 vertical feet.

The run down to Millcreek includes a pleasant north-facing slope with widely-spaced trees, a flat section, and then 1000 feet of very steep densely-wooded terrain that will challenge even the most capable skier. There are a couple of narrow chutes down through the trees that offer a relatively clear path. Deep untracked snow is important for controlling speed since there is little room to make turns. It's sort of like a roller coaster!

The downhill part of this tour has a vertical drop of 2100 feet over 1.4 miles, followed by a 3.4 mile run along the Millcreek highway.

EAST BRANCH OF ALEXANDER BASIN. By far the best alternative for this canyon is the east branch, which borders Wilson Fork. The ascent route is exactly the same as that described previously for Wilson. You can start at Mill D North or Butler in Big Cottonwood and climb the ridge to the peak at the top of Wilson. The hike from Mill D is 4.7 miles with 2600 vertical feet.

The east branch of Alexander starts at this peak. The safest descent is along the ridge on either side of the open area at the top and then down through the trees to the main part of the basin. (See Fig. 4-7.) Below that is the flat area and the steep drop to the Millcreek highway. Distance from the top of Wilson is 1.9 miles with 2400 feet of elevation difference.

UPPER ALEXANDER BASIN. Figs. 4-4 and 4-7 show two views of the approach to the upper end of the basin. It is simply an extension of the climb to the top of Wilson Fork. The ridge between these two points is quite flat but has a couple of narrow rocky spots that may require removal of skis*. Total climb from Mill D North is 2600 feet over 5.1 miles.

The photo of Alexander illustrates the hazards awaiting anyone who challenges the upper headwall. There are a few trees but they offer little protection on such a steep slope. The greatest exposure is from the cliffs on the west side of the basin that rise more than 800 feet to the summit of Gobblers Knob. The skier who can't resist will—hopefully—have a 2.1 mile run down to the highway. □

---

*It is advisable to tie your skies to yourself when scrambling up or down the rocks. A dropped ski might not be found until summer.

5 NEFFS CANYON

Neffs Canyon, unlike its neighbors to the south, has not yet been violated by civilization.

The early pioneers, John Neff in particular, utilized some of the canyon's timber resources, but the cutting was done with an amazing degree of moderation and self control. After only a partial defloration of the virgin hillsides, the sheep and cattle raisers sought greener pastures elsewhere in the Wasatch. Several mining incursions have been made, but, unlike Bingham Canyon in the Oquirrhs, they were abandoned before the area was totally disemboweled.

For many decades, Neffs Canyon has remained relatively untouched. No cabins or condominiums protrude from its wooded slopes. No summits have been decapitated for ski lift towers. Not a single summer arts festival has been promoted here, and the Utah Symphony has yet to play its first controversial note along the ancient streambed.

Neffs is best known to a handful of spelunkers, for whom the canyon is Mecca, to be exalted twice daily and to be visited at least once in each lifetime. One of the world's deepest caves lies nestled in the oak brush part way up the drainage.

Neffs is the smallest and shortest of the canyons along the Wasatch Front. The drainage is only 3.7 miles long. It starts at the eastern edge of the Mount Olympus Cove subdivision, at an elevation of 5600 feet, and climbs to an unnamed 9,776 foot peak

Figure 5-1—Neffs Canyon is best known as the home of one of the deepest caves in North America. It drops a total of 1170 feet below the ground, and has rooms that are more than 100 feet tall.

common to Neffs, Millcreek, and Big Cottonwood Canyons.

The north flank of Neffs has no side drainages and is generally covered with thick scrub oak. Two small side canyons come into the main drainage from the south. Norths Fork, named after one of the early pioneers who cut timber in the area, lies directly beneath the rocky northeast slopes of Mount Olympus. Thomas Fork, the second side canyon above the Cove, is longer but not quite as steep. Both are heavily wooded in their lower sections.

Unlike Millcreek and Big Cottonwood, Neffs Canyon does not have a great variety of ski touring possibilities. This canyon contains no routes suitable for the beginner, but does provide opportunities for those with intermediate and advanced capabilities. Routes into this canyon are divided into two categories: Intermediate Tours and "Olympian" Tours.

The intermediate routes are all quite challenging, since they end on a narrow trail through otherwise impenetrable brush. They have no severe exposure to avalanche hazard, however, and allow the option of turning back at any point. Unless one crosses to or from Millcreek or Big Cottonwood Canyon, no car shuttle is necessary. The tourer should be aware that the overall difficulty of a Neffs trip depends to a large extent upon the snow conditions at low elevations. January is often the best month for skiing in this canyon.

The "Olympian" tours require a greater degree of commitment than most advanced outings described in this book. In addition to the usual steepness and avalanche factors, they have the added complexity of hiking and rock scrambling. Tours on Mount Olympus range from the "sublime" (such as a descent of Thomas Fork) to the "suicidal" (such as the couloirs pictured at the beginning of this chapter). The latter require *extremely precise* skiing ability and nerves of steel. A current will and standby ambulance might also be a good idea.

INTERMEDIATE TOURS

There are several possibilities for an intermediate tourer in Neffs Canyon. The "standard" route follows the road and trail along the main drainage to the upper bowl and back. One can also climb Thomas Fork and ski back down. Another possibility is a run down Neffs after climbing to the top from Millcreek or from Big Cottonwood Canyon.

Standard Neffs Canyon Tour

All tours from the bottom of Neffs start at White Reservoir, which is in White Park at the top of White Way.† The most complex part of these trips is the drive from the city to the reservoir, through an upper-middle-class housing development known as Mount Olympus Cove. Most of this subdivision can be avoided by traveling along Wasatch Boulevard to 3800 South. This street is then followed eastward for 0.3 mile until it intersects Park View Drive (3700 East). Park View Drive is followed for about 1.2 miles in a winding south-easterly direction until it intercepts Park Terrace Drive. Turn east onto Park Terrace and follow it past a "Dead End" sign until it is intercepted by White Way.

---

†At the top of White Way there used to stand a home known locally as the "White House", which is no longer there. Greek legend recalls that the house was struck by lightning and burned to the ground as a result of Zeus's displeasure at the Emperor's pardon of a former ruler who had been accused of "high crimes and misdemeanors" and of "preventing, obstructing, and impeding the administration of justice."

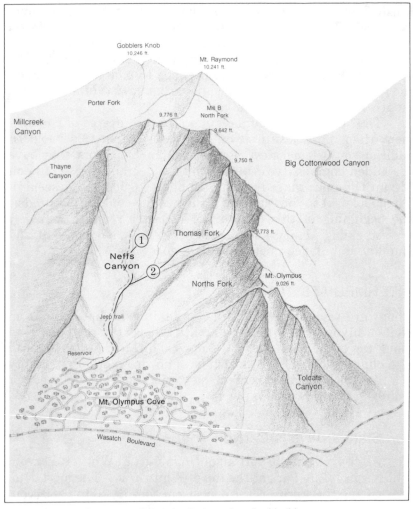

Figure 5-2—The intermediate tours that are described in this chapter all involve a descent of the jeep road in lower Neffs Canyon. The numbered routes are (1) Upper Neffs and (2) Thomas Fork.

White Way is the right way to the reservoir which is enclosed by a fence just left of pavement's end. This is a popular necking area, but early in the day there should be plenty of room to park your car for ski touring.

A jeep road goes southeasterly from the chain link fence around White Reservoir. After 0.5 mile the road turns to the left and crosses the stream. The trail into Norths Fork branches to the right at this point. The road parallels the stream for 1.3

Figure 5-3—Although snow conditions are frequently marginal at lower elevations, upper Neffs Canyon has some good skiing terrain. Note the pipeline on the north side of the canyon that bypasses the brush in the bottom of the drainage.

miles, crossing it twice more. About 150 yards past the final stream crossing, the jeep road ends and a hiking trail begins.

The start of the hiking trail is ill defined, especially during winter. It traverses a very short distance directly up a steep slope just to the right of the end of the road.* At the top of the

---

*This trail is on the south side of the stream, but the U.S.G.S. quadrangle shows it on the north side. What is indicated on the map is actually the route of an abandoned water pipeline, which is a good descent route from Neffs' upper meadows.

slope the trail turns into a deep rut. This portion is followed for about 0.3 mile through a dense forest (prominently visible at the bottom right of Fig. 5-3) until the terrain opens along the bottom of two slopes of moderate steepness. The trail is usually lost (or abandoned) here. This is no problem since at this point the timber and brush are reasonalby sparse. A gentle traverse to the right takes you to the top of a ridge which you can follow for 0.3 mile.

At the end of this secondary ridge, you can angle downward a short distance into some open areas along the bottom of the canyon. The remainder of the trip to the Neffs/Big Cottonwood divide follows the open slopes near the canyon bottom. From White Reservoir to the Big Cottonwood divide is 3.7 miles and 3,600 vertical feet. If you choose to ascend the 9,776 foot un-named peak common to Neffs, Millcreek, and Big Cottonwood Canyons, simply stay to the left as illustrated by the dashed line in the photograph. From White Reservoir to the peak is 3.9 miles with 4,200 feet of elevation gain.

Two descent variations are possible from the Neffs/Big Cottonwood divide back to the starting point. The first retraces the route through the open slopes to the base of the secondary ridge. Instead of climbing back onto this ridge, one should remain on the north side of the canyon above the stream gully. The old pipeline track footnoted earlier is soon intercepted. It rejoins the jeep trail near its end. The second descent route follows some well sheltered, semi-open slopes and depressions just west of the Neffs/Big Cottonwood divide and eventually joins the pipeline route near the secondary ridge.

From the top of the 9,776 foot peak, it is also possible to ski into Porter Fork of Millcreek Canyon. From the summit one can descend along the ridge to the north for about 0.7 mile and then ski down into the Porter drainage. This area is described in more detail in Chapter 5.

Upper Neffs from Big Cottonwood Canyon

The Neffs/Big Cottonwood ridge can be reached from the "S"-curve of the Big Cottonwood highway by ascending either branch of Mill B North Fork. The east branch ends at the divide mentioned in the previous section. The west branch leads to the top of Thomas Fork. Snow conditions on the north side of Big Cottonwood Canyon are usually marginal, often suncrusted, icy, or lacking snow entirely. Except for the first 0.3 mile, no trail exists and the route goes through alternating sections of rock bands and brush. About two miles and 600 feet of elevation

Figure 5-4—Mill B North Fork can be used as an access route for upper Neffs.

are saved by using this approach, but the overall time spent may be greater than on the standard tour. Fig. 5-4 may be used to help pick a route.

Upper Neffs from Millcreek Canyon

The upper part of Neffs Canyon is adjacent to Porter Fork in the Millcreek drainage. An approach from that direction is at least as good as the standard route up Neffs, so it is a reasonable alternative. Details of the climb to the top are found in Chapter 4, but it generally follows a ridge that ends at the 9,776

Figure 5-5—This view of the Salt Lake Valley from Upper Neffs clearly shows why ski tourers like to get as high as possible.

foot peak. This variation of the Neffs tour only saves 400 feet of vertical (3800 feet instead of 4200) but the snow on the northeast-facing slopes of Porter is often much better than that in Neffs, particularly at low elevations. Another advantage of not hiking up Neffs is that all the snow will be left on the trail to slow down your descent.

Thomas Fork

Considerably more exciting and picturesque than the standard Neffs Canyon tour is the ascent of Thomas Fork. From the top of the highest point reached (Peak 9,750 feet on the maps) there is a good view of the double snow plumes from the

Peak (El. 9750 ft.)   Peak (El. 9773 ft.)

Thomas Fork

Figure 5-6—Thomas Fork has two good touring routes, but both end up in thick oak brush at the bottom.

twin summits of Mount Olympus. Further west one can contemplate the entire panorama of the Salt Lake Valley with the Oquirrh Mountains and the Great Salt Lake in the distance. Punctuating this magnificent view are the double plumes from the twin smoke stacks belonging to Kennecott Copper Corporation.

Thomas Fork is a little shorter, steeper, and more difficult than the standard tour. The route is shown in Fig. 5-6. It is 3.6 miles long and requires an elevation gain of 4,200 ft. As in the previous tour, one starts at White Reservoir and follows the jeep road past its junction with Norths Fork at the first crossing of the streambed. About 0.75 mile beyond the junction, to the right of the jeep road, is an "impenetrable" oak grove located atop an ancient alluvial fan. Leave the road here and head almost directly south into the grove. No ski area developers cleared the willows and oak, so considerable ingenuity, persistence, and strength are required to penetrate the brush. After 0.5 mile of bushwacking, the terrain becomes more open and manageable. This point is clearly visible at the extreme bottom of Fig. 5-6. From here, the route becomes obvious, basically following the line on the photograph.

There are only two steep areas on this entire tour which require avalanche precautions. The first is the moderately steep, semi-wooded slope in the lower section of the photo. The second steep area (not visible in the photo) is a small bowl just below the summit of the 9,750 foot peak which is the destination of the tour. This bowl can be avoided by staying on a steep, tree-covered ridge just to the right of the bowl.

Descent of Thomas Fork is relatively straightforward. Besides skiing along the upward route, only one simple alternative exists. This is marked in Fig. 5-6. The lower portion of this descent is extremely steep, especially the area marked (A) in the illustration, so it should be attempted only under the safest snow conditions.

OLYMPiAN TOURS

Unlike its counterpart in Greece, Utah's Mount Olympus has lacked the ingredients from which great legends arise. With discovery of the area by ski tourers, this will undoubtedly change, for some of the outings to be described in this section are almost guaranteed to elevate mere mortals to deity, and to start Utah's second mythological chain.

There are three practical tours in the Mount Olympus area. With reference to Fig. 5-8 these are: (1) Mount Olympus/Norths Fork, (2) Mount Olympus/Thomas Fork, (3) the Mount Olympus Couloir. In addition, a series of "memorial couloirs" exist along the northeast side of the mountain. These will be described briefly at the end of this chapter for those carefree tourers who have no mortgages and maintain no mistresses.

All the Olympian tours start from the regular Forest

Figure 5-7—Unpersuaded by arguments of "a broadened tax base," "greater employment opportunities for his fellow dieties," and "the need to balance economic and environmental considerations," an enraged Zeus banishes two executives of the Chamber of Commerce who proposed to erect a scenic tramway and revolving restaurant atop the summit of Mt. Olympus.

Service "Tolcats Canyon" trailhead along Wasatch Blvd. at about 60th South. Ample parking space is available along the west side of the highway.

Norths Fork from Mount Olympus

From the sign reading: "Tolcats Canyon—Private Property —Travel Restricted to Trail—National Forest Land ¼ Mile", the trail bears north and east along the western and northern boundaries of a fenced area. Once past the fence the trail zig zags back and forth through open, grassy slopes for the first mile. It then traverses for 0.25 mile directly into Tolcats Canyon, where a streambed is intercepted. After crossing the stream the trail ascends a steep, 0.25 mile section known fondly as "blister hill", crosses a ridge, and traverses farther southeast toward a second stream channel. For the next 0.4 mile the trail ascends a relatively steep, scrub-covered slope following the drainage of the second stream channel. At the top is a broad, evergreen-covered plateau (visible at the bottom right of Fig. 5-9) which serves as an excellent picnic place during the summer. The 9,026

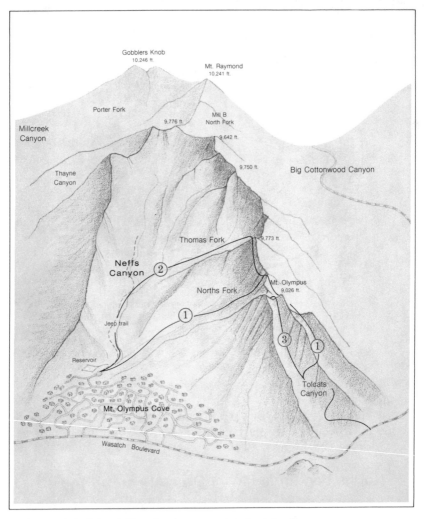

Figure 5-8—Several Olympian tours are described for the skier who enjoys hiking, rock scrambling, and extremely steep downhill runs. Possibilities are (1) Norths Fork, (2) Thomas Fork and (3) the Mount Olympus couloir.

foot south summit of Mount Olympus juts 500 feet above to the north.

The top of Norths Fork is about 0.4 mile east of the plateau. It lies at the saddle between Mount Olympus and a rocky, unnamed summit. One can traverse slightly upward beneath the face of the peak as shown in Fig. 5-9 , or descend about 100 feet, then traverse and climb some moderately steep slopes to the

Figure 5-9 — Norths Fork and Thomas Fork are reached from the Mount Olympus trail by traversing south of the peak from the shoulder to the pass at the head of Norths Fork.

pass. The first alternative has some short rock scrambles, while the latter has some avalanche potential, so take your pick! Wasatch Blvd. to Norths Fork saddle is 3 miles with 3,800 feet of vertical.

Even though it is only 1.8 miles in length and 3,000 vertical feet, the descent of Norths Fork can at times be very difficult. The upper section is steep and avalanche prone. The lower areas are extremely brushy and may contain marginal snow. A good route is along the eastern side until the canyon narrows at the bottom. Here, one can cross the stream to its western side and intercept a steep, curvy foot trail, which joins the main Neffs Canyon jeep road leading to White Reservoir.

Thomas Fork from Mount Olympus

Thomas Fork is just east of Norths, so the climbing route is identical to that just described. From the saddle at the top of Norths Fork, drop down about 200 vertical feet and traverse directly east a few hundred yards to the base of a steep cliff band. If the cliff harbors no severe avalanche slab, proceed to traverse under it, staying as close to the trees as necessary. Once past this area, continue to traverse eastward several hundred yards to the base of an open slope. Ascent of this slope puts one at the top of Thomas Fork. Both the cliff band and the open slope are clearly visible in Fig. 5-9, which shows the route just described. The top of the open slope is at an elevation of 8,800 feet providing a 3,200 foot, 2.5 mile descent into the main canyon.

The alternatives for skiing down Thomas Fork were described in an earlier section.

Mount Olympus Couloir

The Mount Olympus Couloir is one of the steepest and most challenging ski runs in the Wasatch. It involves an ascent, via Tolcats Canyon, to the saddle between the north and south summits of Mount Olympus and a descent, via a steep couloir, into Norths Fork.

This tour starts at Wasatch Blvd. and follows the Mount Olympus trail until its first crossing of the Tolcats Canyon streambed. From here, rather than crossing the stream and ascending "blister hill", the streambed is followed directly up to the 8,800 foot saddle between the summits. It is about a mile and 2,500 vertical feet from the stream to the saddle, giving this section an average angle of about 30 degrees. The steep upper portion of Tolcats Canyon is shown in Fig. 5-10A. It can be ascended either by traversing among the trees or by zig-zagging in the open slopes visible in the photograph. Needless to say, this route should not be attempted under uncertain avalanche conditions.

At the top of the saddle there is ample room to relax and ponder the descent route, and to question seriously your reasons for being there. (Wasatch Blvd. to the saddle: 2.3 miles, 3,900 feet.)

The descent into Norths Fork is probably the simplest and least complicated to be described in this book. It is straight, it is narrow, it is short, and it is steep! The initial 1,300 vertical feet of the couloir is more than 40°. Its simplicity is illustrated in Fig. 5-10B. After skiing down the couloir, simply follow the route

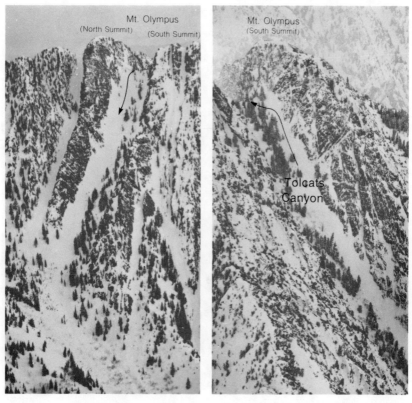

Mt. Olympus
(North Summit) (South Summit)

Mt. Olympus
(South Summit)

Tolcats
Canyon

B   **A**

Figure 5-10—(a) Upper Tolcats is the ascent route to the saddle between the two peaks of Mount Olympus. (b) The couloir on the north side of that saddle is an excellent run for a qualified downhill skier.

described previously for Norths Fork.

The Memorial Couloirs

It is apparent from Fig. 5-10B and the photograph at the beginning of this chapter that there are several couloirs on either side of the main Olympus couloir which are straighter, narrower, and steeper than the one just described. They are presently called the "memorial couloirs." A name will be inserted before "memorial" in honor of the first tourer to perish there. These couloirs will not be named after those who survive them, but the authors will happily include their narratives in further editions of this guide. □

6 BIG COTTONWOOD CANYON

The ski touring terrain in Big Cottonwood Canyon is the most varied and also the most accessible in the Wasatch Mountains. Several beginner outings, mostly near the head of the canyon, have been described in Chapter 3. Redman Campground, Silver Lake, Lower Silver Fork, Mill F East Fork, Lake Solitude, Brighton Lakes, and Snake Creek Pass are all suitable areas for skiers who have not yet gained enough experience to try the more difficult slopes. The intermediate and advanced tours in Big Cottonwood Canyon are the subject of this chapter.

Intermediate ski tours are described first, starting with Catherine Pass, and going westward to Twin Lakes Pass and Mount Wolverine, Mill F South, Honeycomb, Silver Fork, Lower Days Fork, Cardiff Fork and Lower Mineral Fork. On the north side of the canyon are Beartrap Fork, Butler Fork, and Mill A Gulch. The tours are *not* listed in order of increasing or decreasing difficulty. Rather, the descriptions are in a geographical progression to allow easy reading. Often, a tour is simply an extension of others, so more than one section must be read in order to get complete information on the entire route. For example, the Silver Fork tour is described in detail only from

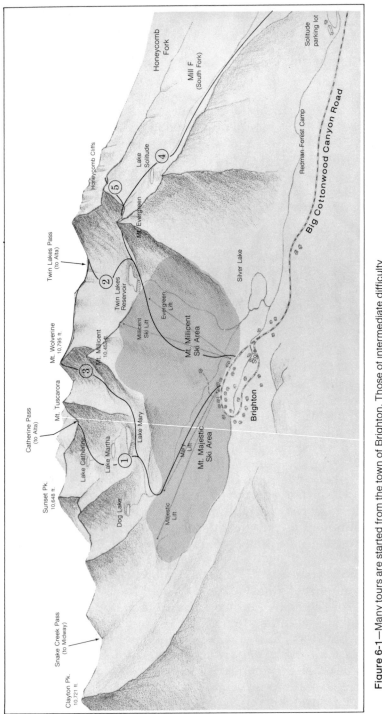

Figure 6-1—Many tours are started from the town of Brighton. Those of intermediate difficulty described in this chapter are (1) Catherine Pass, (2) Twin Lakes Pass, (3) Mount Wolverine, (4) Mill F South Fork, and (5) Honeycomb Fork. Twin Lakes Pass also provides access to Silver Fork and Days Fork.

Twin Lakes Pass; a preceding section covered the Twin Lakes Pass tour. Similarly, Mill A Gulch is most conveniently approached from Butler Fork, so both sections contain important information for someone desiring to ski down Mill A.

Advanced tours in Big Cottonwood Canyon are principally on the south slopes. Days Fork, Lake Blanche, Mineral Fork, and Broads Fork all have runs that will challenge even the expert downhill skier. Mount Raymond and Gobbler's Knob are also very steep and hazardous at the higher elevations.

Many tours in this chapter have routes suggested for the climb that are not the same as for the descent. There are two reasons for this. Often, a significant vertical advantage can be gained by starting and ending in different places. For example, the Days Fork tour could be done from the bottom with over 3,000 feet of elevation change both ways, but the total climb from Alta or Brighton is less than 2,000 feet (or approximately 1,000 ft. if the Evergreen Lift is used). The tour is admittedly longer, but the ascent is easier. The second reason for different routes is safety. The steep slopes and open bowls that provide the best downhill skiing are also the most hazardous. A tourer should minimize his exposure to avalanche danger, so traversing back and forth to get up such an area should be avoided whenever possible. In the back country, discretion is the better part of skiing.

INTERMEDIATE TOURS

Catherine Pass

The most popular skiing and hiking route between Brighton and Alta goes over Catherine Pass. It is easily reached from either side with about 1,400 feet of climbing in relatively safe and moderate terrain. Catherine Pass and the lake just to the east were named for Catherine Brighton, a wife of William Brighton, who lived in upper Big Cottonwood Canyon for the last four decades of the nineteenth century. They ran a hotel and store, and rented cottages to people visiting the area. Brighton was a popular resort spot even then.

The route to Catherine Pass is an extension of the tour to Lake Mary described in Chapter 3. The simplest way from the parking lot at Brighton is to climb through the trees or on the ski trail to the right of the Mary Lift. (Or you could take the lift for the price of a single ride ticket.) About .2 mile above the top of the lift, the ski trail takes a sharp bend to the left. At this point, *go to the right* traversing up the hill through the trees,

Figure 6-2—Catherine Pass from Brighton is a pleasant tour over moderate terrain that takes the skier past all four of the lakes that are popular destinations for summer hikes.

and then follow the drainage to the Lake Mary dam. Above the lake, stay to the left and climb along the ridge overlooking Dog Lake until the ridge gets steep and rocky. Bear right and follow a gentle, upward traverse to Lake Catherine. There are some very exposed slopes on the left in this area which are avoided by taking a lower line through the large fir trees as shown in Fig. 6-2.

The most hazardous part of this ski tour is between Lake Catherine and the pass. The steep slopes on Sunset Peak to the left and Mount Tuscarora to the right are all prone to avalanche.

122

Figure 6-3 — Lake Catherine is surrounded by very steep slopes, so the route to the pass must be chosen carefully. Notice the small ridge that can provide protection from avalanche paths coming off Sunset Peak and Mount Tuscarora.

Just below the pass, however, there is a small secondary ridge that goes straight down toward the lake. (See Fig. 6-3.) This provides the tourer with a relatively safe approach when the snow is stable. It is best to stop at the lake when avalanche conditions are particularly bad. The total distance from Brighton to the pass is about 2.2 miles.

The safest descent from Catherine Pass is the route just described, but there are other variations for those desiring a steeper and longer run in the powder.

One alternative is to follow the ridge to the south toward Sunset Peak. On either side of the summit there are slopes running all the way to Lake Catherine which can be skied if conditions permit. This area is extremely hazardous and usually must be saved until spring.

Another possible return route is to climb the ridge north of the pass and go over the top of Tuscarora to Mount Wolverine. The lower part is often quite rocky and brushy, but the run down Mt. Wolverine to Brighton can be worth the effort. Details of the possibilities from Mount Wolverine to Brighton can be found in a later section of this chapter.

The third alternative is to ski down the west side of the pass to Alta and return to Brighton via Grizzly Gulch and Twin Lakes Pass. Chapter 7 has the information on these tours.

Figure 6-4—Twin Lakes Pass can be approached from the dam by a relatively safe route along the power line. (Fig. 6-6 shows this from another angle.) The traverse around Wolverine Cirque from the Millicent lift is much more exposed to avalanche hazard. Also shown are touring routes in upper Mill F South.

Twin Lakes Pass

The second ski touring alternative between Brighton and Alta is Twin Lakes Pass, where the power line crosses the ridge between Big and Little Cottonwood Canyons. In the old mining days, the road over Twin Lakes Pass was a heavily traveled route both winter and summer. It was common for sightseers to make a round trip by going from Salt Lake to Brighton, then over the pass and down Little Cottonwood Canyon. The pass is only about 1,200 vertical feet from Brighton or Alta, with a climb of about 1.7 miles from either town.

A skier headed for Twin Lakes Pass from Brighton will find it difficult to avoid the downhill traffic at the ski area unless he condescends to ride a chairlift. If this alternative is chosen, the Evergreen Lift, which ends at the Twin Lakes dam, is the best choice. It has less vertical rise than the Millicent Lift (1,600 versus 1,100 ft.), but the route to the pass from the top of Evergreen is much safer. (See Fig. 6-4.)

The tourer who elects to begin his trip at the parking lot can start out to the left of the Millicent Lift and follow the trail that winds its way upward, eventually crossing back under Millicent, and ending at the top of Evergreen. It is usually safest to stay in the unpacked snow beside the downhill trails when climbing at a ski area.

From the Twin Lakes dam, the best touring route to the pass goes across or around the lake and intersects the power line. There are some good terrain features that can provide protection most of the way from this point. The power line is a good guide, since it stays generally in the trees or along the top of a minor ridge. (Note the hazardous avalanche zones that a tourer must cross if he strays too far in either direction.)

Many alternatives exist for the return from Twin Lakes Pass. The simplest, of course, is to return the same way. Several other possibilities are described in later sections on Mount Wolverine, Grizzly Gulch (Chapter 7), Silver Fork, and Days Fork. A pleasant round trip tour is to go down Grizzly Gulch to Alta, then ski back to Brighton via Albion Basin and Catherine Pass. One other variation when conditions are very stable is to traverse to the south and ski the lower part of Wolverine Cirque as shown in Fig. 6-4.

Mount Wolverine

The highest of the peaks that lie between Brighton and Alta is Mount Wolverine. It is formed by the intersection of three ridges, one from Twin Lakes Pass and one from each of its sisters, Mount Millicent and Mount Tuscarora. At 10,800 feet, it stands above all others at the head of Big Cottonwood Canyon. Wolverine is a very rugged peak that is often exposed to severe wind and weather. Thus, snow conditions at the higher elevations are usually very difficult, making this one of the most challenging intermediate tours in the Wasatch. It is an alpine tour and not suggested for cross-country skis.

There are three recommended routes to the summit of Mount Wolverine. All are along ridges which have steep sections and which often have rocky areas where the wind has eroded the snow away. In fact, you may have to remove your skis and walk in some places. Don't forget to stay away from the edge of cornices since it is difficult to tell how far they overhang. Also, remember that the windward side of a ridge is generally less susceptible to avalanche danger.

Figure 6-5—Mount Wolverine is the highest peak at the end of Big Cottonwood Canyon. When the snow has accumulated enough to cover the rocks, there are challenging intermediate powder runs down to the lakes.

FROM TWIN LAKES PASS. The easiest approach to Mount Wolverine is from Twin Lakes Pass, which is accessible from Brighton, as described previously, and from Grizzly Gulch (see Chapter 7). From the pass, simply follow the ridge south to the summit. Total distance from either Alta or Brighton is about 3 miles with a climb of 2,100 feet.

FROM CATHERINE PASS. The second alternative is to climb the ridge to the north from Catherine Pass over the top of Mount Tuscarora. One route to the pass has been described in this chapter, and another is found in Chapter 7. The total distance to Mount Wolverine is about the same as the Twin Lakes route, but the ridge above Catherine Pass is often more difficult to maneuver.

FROM THE MILLICENT LIFT. The third variation is to climb the ridge from the top of the Millicent ski lift to the summit of Mount Millicent, then continue on to Wolverine. This is the most direct route, about a mile shorter than the others, but also the steepest and rockiest of the three. Its one "salvation" is that half of the work can be eliminated by riding the chair lift.

Two variations are described for the trip down Mount Wolverine. Either way can be quite rocky early in the winter, so the tour is best saved for later in the year. The avalanche hazard also dictates that this area be avoided until the deep, early-season snows have stabilized. Fig. 6-5 shows the possibilities.

The safest descent route is from the saddle between Mount Wolverine and Mount Tuscarora. A line of trees that goes down toward Millicent provides protection in the upper section. Below these trees the terrain flattens out, and it is best to bear right, as illustrated in the photograph, following the wooded areas and ridges near the avalanche gully under Mount Tuscarora. At the point overlooking the Brighton lakes, bear right again for the final descent to Lake Martha. This part is the most exposed to avalanche danger, so it is important to avoid the steep slopes coming off Tuscarora. From the lake, the tourer has the option of skiing over Catherina Pass to Alta or continuing down to Brighton.

The second variation is more hazardous, but there are some nice, steep areas for the powder lover's enjoyment. The bowl at the top of Wolverine is often quite wind-packed, but on a good day it can be a superb run from the summit. Stay to the left at the bottom of the bowl and drop into the gully that starts at the saddle between Wolverine and Millicent. This gully is skiable all the way to Lake Mary, but the lower section is steep and can be dangerous in unstable snow conditions.

Mill F South Fork

The ski tour into the bottom of Mill F South as far as Lake Solitude is a popular beginner outing (Chapter 3), but the upper section of the canyon has some steeper slopes for more advanced skiers. This is a very accessible area, particularly for the tourer who decides to use the Evergreen Lift at Brighton. A round trip can be done in a couple of hours if the snow isn't too deep. Total climb from Brighton is 900 vertical feet (only 300 feet from the top of the lift).

Figure 6-6—The top of Mill F South is an easy traverse from the Twin Lakes dam, and the ridge overlooking Honeycomb is just a short climb from there. The route to Twin Lakes Pass is also shown.

The easiest route to the upper part of Mill F South Fork ascends from Brighton to the saddle above Twin Lakes that overlooks Lake Solitude. The tourer can hike up the downhill ski trails (see the Twin Lakes Pass section for details) or take the Evergreen Lift to the Twin Lakes dam. The short climb from there can be done by heading directly toward the pass, or if the avalanche situation is particularly bad, it is safer to traverse back and forth in the open area near the saddle (Fig. 6-6).

There are two alternatives for the 600 foot descent to Lake Solitude. The safest and easiest way is to traverse from the saddle up and across to the west side of the canyon where the terrain is not as steep. (See Fig. 6-7.) You will cross several open areas in the upper section that look inviting, but they lead to a series of cliffs and extremely steep slopes just above the lake.

Figure 6-7—Mill F South and Honeycomb Fork are both quite short tours that offer a considerable amount of downhill skiing for very little climbing effort. This is particularly true if one of the Brighton lifts is used.

The west wall of the canyon rises very sharply and should be avoided, so the best route is in the trees adjacent to the obvious avalanche paths off the rocks above. Be alert for vertical mine shafts in upper Mill F South; there are several that remain open all winter. A road provides a good path for the last hundred feet to the lake.

The more challenging possibility from the pass to Lake Solitude is to ski straight down on the east side of the canyon.

129

There are two steep, narrow chutes in the trees to the right that are sheltered from wind and sun where good powder snow can usually be found. Avalanche hazard is often very high, since this area is very slow to stabilize, but it's a good run for the competent skier who is willing to take some risk.

Below Lake Solitude, you can stay on the right side of the canyon and traverse about 1.5 miles around to Brighton, or you can ski straight down to the Solitude ski area.

Honeycomb Fork

Honeycomb Fork is actually a branch of Silver Fork that intersects the main canyon just above the Big Cottonwood highway. Its name comes from the cliffs on the west side of the fork that can be observed from the road just below the Silver Fork Lodge. These rocky precipices are a white limestone formation pocketed with thousands of holes that have developed over the years as water percolated down through openings in the stone. The cliffs are truly "honeycombed."

The Honeycomb ski tour can be done from the bottom via Silver Fork, or a 700 ft. elevation advantage can be gained by starting at Brighton.

HONEYCOMB VIA SILVER FORK. This alternative is best for the tourer who wants to avoid the steep avalanche-prone slopes at the top of Honeycomb Fork. A good route into the lower part of the fork starts at the lower Solitude ski area parking lot (see Silver Fork section in Chapter 3) and follows the road through the summer home area into Silver Fork. About ½ mile up the canyon, the Honeycomb drainage comes in from the left. The aspens are quite thick near the bottom, but there is a good road going up the right side of the fork which you can follow if your wax is working properly. When the terrain becomes too steep, or you've had enough exercise, you can turn around and go back down.

HONEYCOMB FROM BRIGHTON. The easiest approach to the top of Honeycomb Fork is from the base of the Evergreen Lift at Brighton. A single ride pass or a short climb up the ski area gets you to the Twin Lakes dam. (See the Twin Lakes Pass section in this chapter.) The route from the dam starts the same as the Mill F tour described previously. Simply traverse from there to the saddle overlooking Lake Solitude, and then continue climbing to the low point in the west ridge of upper Mill F (Fig. 6-4 and 6-6). That is the head of Honeycomb Fork, and is 1,200 feet above the parking lot.

The pass is a good place for a lunch stop where you have a superb view of the cliffs that are often capped with cornices overhanging twenty feet or more. A pair of Golden Eagles have been nesting in the rocks near here in recent years. If they haven't been rendered inoperative by local "sportsmen", you might be treated to a gliding show as you relax before skiing down to your car.

The downhill run to lower Solitude from the top of Honeycomb is 1,900 feet and 3.5 miles. The upper 400 feet is on very steep, open slopes where avalanches are quite common. The area under the cliffs is exposed to the most hazard, so it is wise to stay away from the left side of the canyon in the top section. There are good powder runs on the right side and down the middle, but the skier who isn't able to stay in the fall line will have to take a traverse to the right to avoid the dangerous area under the cliffs. Be alert for the vertical mine shaft at the bottom of the upper bowl.

Below the steep sections at the top, Honeycomb is more gentle and wide enough to allow the tourer to take almost any route down. Fig. 6-7 shows one such possibility. Note that some areas are quite heavily wooded, but open spots can be found to allow pleasant skiing all the way down. The road on the left side at the bottom can be quite fast, especially if several skiers have already packed down the snow, but the trees on either side are spaced widely enough to allow traversing back and forth.

Honeycomb intersects Silver Fork only 0.5 mile above the cabin area, so the run down the road to the highway is simple from there. It is best to park in the lower Solitude parking lot, since the Silver Fork Lodge parking area is open only to customers.

Silver Fork

The history of Silver Fork is full of trauma and tragedy that went hand in hand with the mining boom at the turn of the century. The canyon is dotted with holes left by men who made their fortunes extracting silver ore. Some weren't so fortunate, however. Avalanches took many lives in those years. The hope of overnight wealth overpowered the discretion that should have been foremost in their minds when heavy snows began to accumulate. A reminder of the old mining days that is visible in winter is a tiny cabin perched high on a cliff between the two upper bowls of Silver Fork. Its precarious location and durability stand as a tribute to someone who was determined to beat the odds and make his fortune.

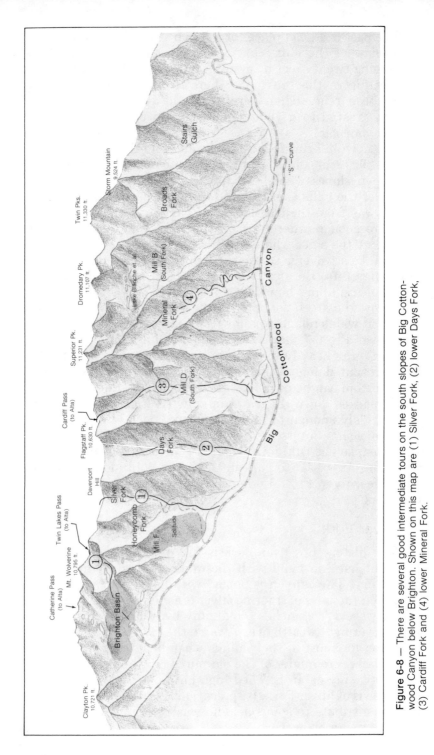

Figure 6-8 — There are several good intermediate tours on the south slopes of Big Cotton-wood Canyon below Brighton. Shown on this map are (1) Silver Fork, (2) lower Days Fork, (3) Cardiff Fork and (4) lower Mineral Fork.

Figure 6-9—Silver Fork is one of the most challenging and dangerous intermediate tours in the Wasatch. Both of the upper bowls are steep and prone to avalanche.

The lower part of Silver Fork was described in Chapter 3 as a good beginner ski tour. An intermediate skier could continue beyond the flat section at the bottom, climb another mile or two, and have an enjoyable run back down without encountering much hazardous terrain. The best climbing route is along the

Figure 6-10—The west bowl of Silver Fork is more hazardous than the other, but there are several lines of trees that offer a degree of protection. This has become a favorite haunt of the helicopter skiers.

west side, as shown in Fig. 6-9, until about 0.3 mile above the large mine on the left. There is a good place to cross the stream at this point, and the terrain is better on the east side beyond that.

Silver Fork can be enjoyed from top to bottom with much less climbing if the tour is started from Brighton or Alta. The pass at the top of the east bowl of Silver Fork is almost exactly the same elevation as Twin Lakes Pass, and only a short traverse away. The total distance down to the highway is about 3.5 miles, and between 2,000 and 2,400 vertical feet, depending upon the route chosen. This is a difficult intermediate tour due to the steepness at the top and the avalanche hazard. Only the most competent skiers should attempt it on cross-country skis.

An earlier section described the climb to Twin Lakes Pass. From Alta, simply ski up Grizzly Gulch to the end; from Brighton, you can take the lift or hike to the Twin Lakes dam, and then follow the power line to the top. The traverse from the pass to the saddle at the top of the east branch of Silver Fork is only about 0.7 mile, but is crosses several avalanche paths. Great care should be taken in this area when snow conditions are at all unstable. To get to the west branch of Silver Fork, simply follow the ridge about 0.7 mile over Davenport Hill to the southwest end of the canyon. Both branches of Silver Fork have good skiing.

The east side is the easier and the safer one, although a tourer should use great caution in either of the upper bowls. There are two possible descent routes in the east branch. You can ski down through the trees below the saddle, or you can traverse to the right across the more difficult areas to get to easier terrain. Both ways expose the tourer to dangerous slopes.

The west bowl of Silver Fork is usually better skiing, but the terrain is more challenging and considerably more hazardous. In fact, a group of eleven experienced tourers were caught in an avalanche here in January 1965. They were skiing down the steep, north-facing slope from the low point in the ridge when a slide released and buried three of them, one of whom was injured seriously. Fig. 6-10 is a closeup that shows the avalanche areas and how they can be avoided. Simply stay on the ridge near the southwest corner of Silver Fork, and ski down among the large trees that can help to hold the snow in place. One should be aware that this bowl is frequented by helicopter skiers who detonate explosive charges in an attempt to knock down impending avalanches.*

The two branches of Silver Fork converge at the bottom of the upper bowls. The best route down from that point is the same as that described for ascending from the bottom. The east side is good for the first half mile or so, then the west side is better below that. The stream bed itself can be good skiing late in the year when snow cover is very heavy, but there are some narrow sections to watch out for.

Lower Days Fork

Days Fork, which empties into Spruces Campground, was another of the very active mining areas in the last part of the nineteenth century. Numerous remnants of its eventful past remain for the summer visitor to enjoy, but in winter, only bumps in the snow can be seen. Days is similar to Silver Fork in many ways. The terrain is extremely steep at the top (so much so that we have classified upper Days Fork as an advanced tour), but the bottom section is more moderate. Part of this canyon would be an excellent beginner tour, except that the lower 300 vertical feet is steep and tricky to negotiate.

Days Fork can be done as an intermediate tour by ascending from the highway to the base of the upper cirque, about 4

---

*Ski tourers have complained of incidents involving helicopters bombing slopes near them. If you should have such an experience, be sure to inform the Forest Service and the County Sheriff of all pertinent details.

Figure 6-11—The lower part of Days Fork has delightfully gentle terrain in all but the bottom part. The upper bowl is very hazardous and is described in a later section.

miles and 2,500 vertical feet. The route to follow is generally along the bottom of the drainage, but the beginning can be a bit confusing. Several streams coming into Big Cottonwood Creek are often open and difficult to cross. The simplest approach

136

from the entrance to Spruces Campground is to bear slightly to the left in the first open area. A bridge spans a small stream on the far side of that first clearing. Beyond a clump of trees is another open area with a pavillion to the left. To avoid having to negotiate any streams, cross this meadow and climb into the canyon by traversing back and forth up the left side until you are above the bottom steep section. If the streams aren't a problem, you can bear right in the clearing near the pavillion, go through an aspen grove, and work your way up the center of the fork.

The easiest descent back to the highway is along the same route as the climb. One alternative visible in Fig. 6-11 is to ski the west side of the canyon on the way down. There are many places where a tourer can traverse up to Reed and Benson Ridge overlooking Cardiff Fork. There is good skiing down the ridge and some excellent runs back into the Days Fork drainage. A particularly good one if the wind hasn't been too active is the last 300 vertical feet along the ridge to the west end of the campground.

Cardiff Fork (Mill D South)

The lower part of Mill D South Fork has some of the best beginner touring terrain in the Wasatch. A skier can go along a road from the Big Cottonwood highway all the way to the Cardiff Mine, which is about 3.5 miles and 1700 vertical feet, without encountering any uncomfortably steep slopes. This canyon also has the advantage of a large parking area plowed at the bottom by the State of Utah. So why didn't we list it in Chapter 3? You guessed it. It's snowmobile heaven! Anyone skiing in lower Cardiff Fork will have to share the trail with his motorized counterpart. Thus, we recommend that the canyon be done as an intermediate tour from Alta to assure at least a couple of miles of challenging but peaceful skiing in the upper section.

Anyone who decides to do this tour from the bottom should be alert for the fork in the road about 0.7 miles from the Big Cottonwood highway. The right fork crosses the Cardiff stream and leads up the canyon, while the left one goes only a short distance and stops. Evidence of an active past is visible all along the route up Mill D South. The area just below Donut Falls used to be known as Taggart Flat, named after a family that was killed in an avalanche during the late nineteenth century. A glance at the steep slopes on the side of Kessler Peak just west of the trail will tell the tourer why that wasn't a good spot

Figure 6-12—The ascent from Alta to Cardiff Pass is best accomplished by following the power line from the Guard Station. The avalanche area to the left should always be avoided. Also visible in the bottom of this photo is the road to Grizzly Gulch and Twin Lakes Pass.

to build a house. The number of deserted buildings in this fork and the size of the nearby tailing piles attest to the extent of mining operations in the area at one time.

The route to Cardiff Pass (or Pole Line Pass) from Alta is well marked by a power line which basically follows a minor ridge as shown in Fig. 6-12. Note the avalanche paths on either side that the careful tourer should always avoid. A good starting point for the climb is the Forest Service Guard Station on the west end of town. A road goes part way up from there and ends

Figure 6-13—Several possibilities exist for the run down Cardiff Fork. The safest and easiest is the east branch in the upper left corner of the photo. The hazards of the west branch are shown in Fig. 6-23 in the Lake Blanche section. The route from Montreal Hill into Mineral Fork is marked in the photo.

at one of the old mines. The climb along the power line is generally quite moderate, although there are a couple of steep sections. The total ascent is about 1400 vertical feet and a bit over a mile.

The run down into Cardiff has many variations as Fig. 6-13 shows. Most of the canyon is quite gentle but the upper bowls have some extremely steep sections which should be avoided unless conditions are particularly stable. The fork is divided into two parts by a ridge that runs about a mile down to the Cardiff mine. The pass is at the top of the east side of the canyon. The easiest descent route into Mill D South is directly below the pass, through the trees and across an open slope to the bottom of the drainage. Even this area is prone to avalanche, so care should be exercised. Another possibility for the east bowl is to follow the ridge south from Cardiff Pass over the first high point and down to the first saddle. The slope below that often has better snow.

The west bowl of Cardiff Fork is one of the most hazardous areas in the Wasatch and should be treated with great respect. The northeast side of Mount Superior, for example, drops more than 1000 feet with an average slope of almost 45°. The Lake Blanche tour described later in the chapter has more information on this area.

The lower part of Cardiff is simply a run down very gentle terrain, along a road to the highway. If more challenge is desired, one can climb to the left from the Cardiff mine to the top of Montreal Hill for a few extra turns before the terrain flattens out.

Lower Mineral Fork

Mineral Fork is very similar to Day's Fork, which was described earlier in the chapter. As its name implies, this canyon was also a center of activity around the turn of the century when visions of gold and silver dominated the minds of hundreds of would-be millionaires. Mineral Fork is the home of the Regulator-Johnson mine, perched high in the upper cirque at an elevation of 10,200 feet in the middle of an active avalanche area. It is truly amazing that such a venture could succeed with the technology that existed at the time.

The top of Mineral is extremely hazardous, as Fig. 6-14 illustrates, but most of the fork is quite heavily wooded. An old mining road climbs gradually along the stream from the highway to the upper bowl. Only the very bottom of the canyon is of sufficient difficulty to preclude a beginner rating for lower Mineral Fork. The bottom section of the road traverses back and forth for about 700 vertical feet before it levels off. Another problem in this area is that the elevation is only about 7000 feet,

Figure 6-14—Lower Mineral Fork is quite heavily wooded and narrow, so the tourer is restricted to an old mining road that intersects the Big Cottonwood highway about 1.5 miles above the S-curve.

so snow conditions are often marginal. The tourer may have to remove his skis and walk, especially when coming down!

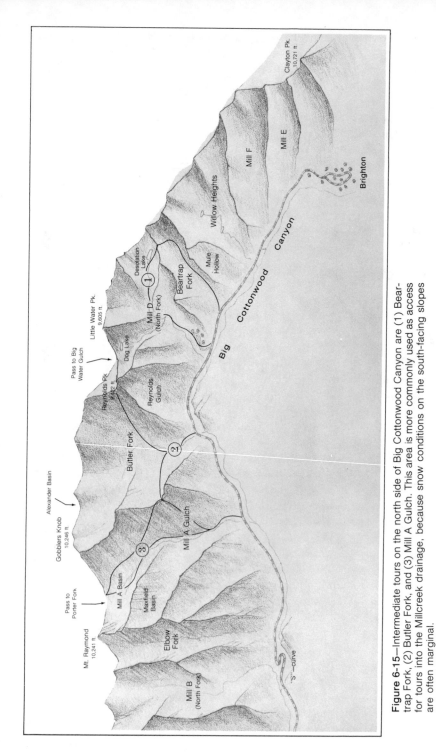

Figure 6-15—Intermediate tours on the north side of Big Cottonwood Canyon are (1) Bear-trap Fork, (2) Butler Fork, and (3) Mill A Gulch. This area is more commonly used as access for tours into the Millcreek drainage, because snow conditions on the south-facing slopes are often marginal.

Above the switchbacks, the Mineral Fork road wanders through a fairly dense oak and aspen forest that allows the tourer few opportunities to deviate. About 2.3 miles from the Big Cottonwood highway, the canyon opens up and gets much steeper. A competent intermediate skier could climb another 1400 vertical feet into the upper cirque, but avalanche hazard becomes an important consideration. The chutes on the west side of the canyon frequently slide all the way to the stream. Total climb from the highway to the base of the cirque is about 4.0 miles and 2900 vertical feet.

Anyone wishing to venture into the upper reaches of Mineral Fork should read the appropriate section later in the chapter under Advanced Tours.

Beartrap Fork

Beartrap Fork is on the north side of Big Cottonwood just below the settlement at Silver Fork. In the 1860's the Littleford family, who lived at the mouth of this fork, reportedly trapped bear in the area. Despite this fact, several summer homes have been built there in recent years. (Apparently the Littlefords got all the bears.) Not many ski tourers venture into Beartrap, probably because parts of it are somewhat narrow and steep, but it is really a delightful area for an intermediate tourer. (See Fig. 6-16.)

The easiest way to do Beartrap is from Desolation Lake, which was described as a beginner tour in Chapter 3. This eliminates climbing the steeper places that might be difficult without skins or just the right wax. To get into the head of Beartrap from Desolation, simply follow the ridge on the west side of the lake to the first low spot. This overlooks an open area that is a good entry point for Beartrap. Beware of the avalanche-prone slopes around Desolation Lake. Total climb from the mouth of Mill D is 4.3 miles and 2200 vertical feet.

Before heading down the canyon, it's worth the time to follow the ridge farther east around the Desolation Lake cirque to the high point overlooking Park City. This is one of the most spectacular panoramas in the Wasatch Mountains. Notable landmarks, going clockwise from the east, include Heber and the Uinta Mountains, the Park City ski area, Brighton ski area, Mount Wolverine, Solitude ski area with Devil's Castle and Sugarloaf beyond, Silver Fork with Mount Baldy and American Fork Twins in the background, Mount Superior, Dromedary, Twin Peaks, the Oquirrh Mountains scarred by Kennecott's

Figure 6-16—Beartrap Fork is most commonly approached from Desolation Lake in upper Mill D North Fork. The peak at the head of Beartrap is a good spot from which to view the Wasatch, Oquirrh, and Uinta Mountains.

"grand canyon" to the west, Mount Raymond, Gobbler's Knob, the Great Salt Lake with Antelope Island, Ben Lomond near Ogden and other northern Wasatch Peaks, Park West ski area with East Canyon Reservoir in the distance, and back to the Uintas. Good place for a camera!

The descent into Beartrap requires no guide. It's quite narrow and wooded in places, so the easiest way down is to ski where the snow is best. The bottom of the canyon is skiable if the snow is deep enough, but some places are too brushy. About halfway down to the highway, the fork widens and becomes relatively flat. If your car is at Mill D, keep to the right near the bottom and you will have to follow the highway only for a mile or so. Total distance of the round trip is 7.4 miles.

If you choose to go up Beartrap instead of Mill D, a good place to begin is just below the Silver Fork area where a road traverses up through the aspens to the summer home area. The

144

Figure 6-17—The east branch of Butler Fork ends at the Big Cottonwood/Millcreek ridge near Reynolds Peak. A popular tour involves traversing across the north slope of Reynolds from Butler to Dog Lake in the Mill D North drainage.

only place that might be confusing is just beyond the flat area that starts about 0.5 miles from the highway. The canyon branches there, and the right branch leads to the ridge overlooking Desolation Lake and Park City. Near the top, the steep slopes on the east side should be avoided, but otherwise there is very little avalanche danger.

Butler Fork/Gobbler's Knob

Butler Fork is on the north side of Big Cottonwood where the canyon starts to bend toward the southeast. It is one of many Wasatch forks named after the operator of a mill or mine that played an important part in its early history. In this case, it was Neri Butler, who ran a steam sawmill in the 1800's. This was one of the areas that provided timber for the Mormon pioneers to build their "promised land" in the wilderness. It is difficult to imagine what these mountains must have been like before tens of millions of board feet of lumber were hauled into the valley.

Butler Fork is a fairly narrow, steep-sided canyon near the

145

bottom, but it soon becomes wider. The fork rises 1700 feet in about 2.3 miles, where it ends at the ridge overlooking Millcreek Canyon just north of Reynolds Peak. The tourer should be aware that a branch of Butler bears to the left about 0.5 miles from the highway and eventually terminates at the ridge overlooking Mill A Basin. Either branch has good skiing, but the main part of the canyon is easier with gentler terrain and more room to maneuver between the aspens.

Several alternatives exist for Butler. The most obvious is to climb up and ski back down. Another possibility is to go up the left branch and down Mill A Gulch (see next section), or continue to the saddle between Gobbler's Knob and Mount Raymond, which is at the head of Porter Fork in Millcreek Canyon (see Chapter 4). The main branch of Butler is commonly used as a route to Alexander Basin or one of the other Millcreek tours described in an earlier chapter. A relatively simple alternative is to climb up the east branch to the top, traverse 0.4 mile through the firs behind Reynolds Peak to Dog Lake, and go down Mill D North Fork. It could just as easily be done in the other direction. (Chapter 3 contains the Dog Lake tours.)

For the ski mountaineer, Butler Fork provides three routes to the 10,246 foot summit of Gobbler's Knob. These really aren't intermediate ski tours, but they are mentioned here for completeness. The peak is at the intersection of three ridges, all of which have some steep and rocky sections. (See Fig. 6-18.) One ridge goes to the saddle below Mount Raymond, one divides the east and west branches of Butler, and the other goes to the head of the east branch. All other routes to or from the summit are exposed to hazardous avalanche areas.

Mill A Gulch/Mount Raymond

John Maxfield operated the first of the sawmills built by the Big Cottonwood Lumber Company, a venture organized by Brigham Young and other prominent pioneers to provide building materials for their growing community. Today the name of Maxfield is more closely associated with the mine discovered by his sons in Mill A Gulch in 1872. It produced a fortune in gold, but before the claim was developed, the Maxfields had the bad luck of selling it for the mere sum of two mules, a wagon, and $80. Somebody really got a deal!

Mill A is a fairly narrow canyon with lots of aspens, but its slope is gradual enough to make the run down quite pleasant. The ascent to the top of the gulch is most easily accomplished via the west branch of Butler Fork for two reasons. There is

Figure 6-18—The west branch of Butler Fork is used primarily for access to Mill A, Mount Raymond, Gobblers Knob, or Porter Fork in Millcreek Canyon. Two descent routes in Mill A Basin are shown in the photo.

more room to traverse back and forth in Butler, and the bottom of Mill A is in a "no parking" zone of the Big Cottonwood highway. You can't leave your car in that area due to avalanche hazard below the gullies marked in Fig. 6-18 and 6-19. The only real danger in the gulch itself is from snow coming from the steep sides into the bottom of the drainage.

There are several options for the descent from Butler. The route shown in Fig. 6-19 drops into the bottom of the gulch and follows it back to the highway. This requires a climb of only 1.6 miles and 1500 vertical feet. An alternative that often has better snow is below the saddle between Gobbler's Knob and Mount Raymond (Fig. 6-18), which is an extra 1.4 miles and 700 feet

Figure 6-19—Mill A Gulch leads to the Big Cottonwood highway from the basin between Gobblers Knob and Mount Raymond. It is usually approached from Butler Fork.

of elevation.

A more advanced tour for the mountaineer is the ridge to the top of Mount Raymond (10,241 feet). This is not a particularly difficult climb, but the descent from the summit might prove more challenging than an intermediate tourer would enjoy. The steep cirque can be a powder hound's delight, but the avalanche hazard is usually too great for this to be a feasible option. You will usually end up following the ridge back to the saddle and dropping into Mill A from there.

ADVANCED TOURS

Big Cottonwood Canyon has an enormous variety of advanced touring terrain. Most of it is located along the south side of the

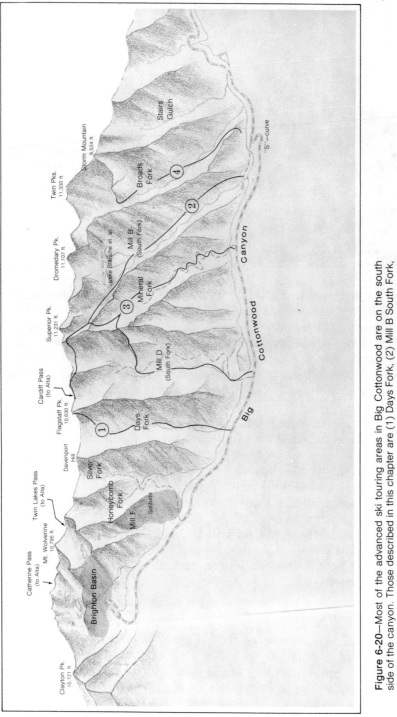

Figure 6-20—Most of the advanced ski touring areas in Big Cottonwood are on the south side of the canyon. Those described in this chapter are (1) Days Fork, (2) Mill B South Fork, (3) Mineral Fork, and (4) Broads Fork. All are extremely steep and hazardous in the upper sections.

Figure 6-21—The safest descent into the cirque at the head of Days Fork is through the trees on the west side. Great care should be exercised regardless of the route chosen.

canyon in the many glacial cirques and forks that originate at the Little Cottonwood divide. Because many of the touring routes into these canyons cross steep, open, north and east-facing slopes whose avalanche conditions are automatically suspect, skiers must be especially aware. So severe is the avalanche danger that at least *23 knowledgeable ski tourers* have been caught and trapped by snow slides in this area during the past decade.

The north side of Big Cottonwood is somewhat more benign. Most of the tours there are rated as beginner or intermediate. The only two difficult tours are Mount Raymond and Gobbler's Knob, which were described briefly in earlier sections.

The simplest and most popular advanced tour in Big Cottonwood Canyon leads directly over Flagstaff Peak from Alta, and down into Day's Fork. The most spectacular series of tours include Mineral Fork, Mill B South Fork (Lake Blanche), and Broad's Fork, as shown schematically in Fig. 6-20. Each successive fork is steeper, longer, and more hazardous than its easterly neighbor.

Days Fork

An earlier section of this chapter described lower Days Fork as an intermediate tour. Fig. 6-21 illustrates that the upper bowl has a much different character. The entire south side is a series of avalanche chutes that the sensible skier would avoid in all but the most stable conditions. The trees on the west side of

150

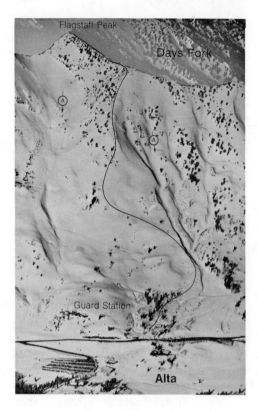

Figure 6-22—The ridge directly above the Alta Lodge is the most direct route to Days Fork. It is important to avoid the avalanche gullies on both sides of this ridge. (Be aware that snow slides have on occasion followed the suggested touring path and done great damage to the lodges below.)

the Days Fork cirque provide some protection for the tourer, but care must always be exercised in the top part of this canyon. The section below the upper cirque is generally quite benign, as mentioned earlier in the chapter. Total run from the top of the canyon is 3150 feet, over 4.1 miles.

Three possibilities are described for the climb to the summit of Flagstaff Peak, which lies at the head of Days Fork.

(1) The safest approach is along the ridge from Twin Lakes Pass. The route is the same as that into Silver Fork, except it is a few hundred yards longer. The tour can be done from Alta or Brighton with a total ascent of 1900 feet in about 4.5 miles. This is quite a long route, but it avoids the steep slopes that must otherwise be climbed.

(2) The most popular route to Flagstaff is shown in Fig. 6-22. A steep ridge from the peak goes straight down into the town of Alta, terminating at the Alta Lodge. The gullies on each side of this ridge should always be avoided; they are the avalanche paths that have repeatedly put Alta in the news. This is a south-facing slope which often stabilizes within a few days of

151

the last storm. In the cold, windy, snowy part of the winter, however, great care should be exercised in any area as exposed as this. When the sun gets higher in the late winter and early spring, this route is at its best.

(3) The third way to Flagstaff is up Days Fork from the Big Cottonwood highway. The only advantage of this alternative is that it eliminates the hitch-hiking or car-spotting of a two-canyon tour. The disadvantages are the distance and elevation of the climb, and the length of time that one is exposed to the avalanche hazard of the upper cirque. Skiing down is dangerous enough, but climbing up is definitely not recommended.

Mill B South Fork (Lake Blanche)

Lake Blanche[†] is considered by many to be among the finest ski tours in the Wasatch Range. Throughout its nearly five mile length, this tour possesses a unique blend of alpine characteristics: jagged summits, treeless cirques, mountain lakes, meadows, and forests. The upper part of the fork is wide open with lots of room for a skier to carve his most graceful turns. The lower section is a steep and narrow hiking trail that can provide even the most experienced ski mountaineer with moments of excitement and amusement (and even despair when the snow is hard and daylight is rapidly disappearing).

There are three common variations to the Lake Blanche tour. One is the "standard" route starting from Alta, and the others are "anti-establishment" alternatives commencing from upper or lower Big Cottonwood Canyon. The latter two will appeal to those who detest traffic jams, high-rise condominiums and the commercial atmosphere of the Alta-Snowbird complex. They also have the advantage of eliminating a car shuttle.

MILL B SOUTH FORK FROM ALTA. The "standard" Lake Blanche ski tour consists of an ascent from Alta to Cardiff Pass, a traverse and climb to the ridge between Mill D South (Cardiff) and Mill B South, and then a descent to Lake Blanche and the S-curve in the Big Cottonwood highway. From the town of Alta, one follows the power line to Cardiff Pass (see Fig. 6-12). Care should be taken to avoid the avalanche-prone slopes on either side of the pole line; it was laid out to avoid avalanches, and the tourer should take advantage of this well-planned ascent route.

From Cardiff Pass there are two common ways to get to

[†] Lake Blanche, along with nearby lakes Lilian and Florence, are rumored to have been named by the early pioneers after three zealous ladies of the late nineteenth century who served law and order by moonlighting as police decoys in nearby mining camps.

"Cardiac Pass",* which is at the head of the east branch of Mill B South Fork. The merits of these and other routes have been examined and extensively debated by avalanche connoisseurs and Forest Service personnel. The general conclusion seems to be that none are particularly safe. In Fig. 6-23, these routes are labeled (1) and (2). Number (3) in the photograph follows the ridge directly to the summit of Mount Superior. Although it is relatively free from avalanche hazard, it is not frequently used because of its steepness and general difficulty.

The two alternatives to be described involve some loss of elevation in order to stay on safer terrain, but the extra climb is well worth the effort. One route drops down into Mill D South and stays below the extremely steep areas, and the other follows the ridge as far as possible and goes above many of the dangerous slopes. Regardless of which of these routes is chosen, the cirque below Cardiac cannot be avoided.

(1) The safest of the two approaches is the lower one.† Unfortunately, it requires the most climbing. From the pass the tourer descends into the fork by angling down and to the left toward the secondary ridge that separates the east and west sides of upper Cardiff. After a short climb to this ridge, the skier again loses elevation and traverses in a westerly direction, being careful to stay well away from the steep slopes that could send "white death" down on an unwary group. The climb into the cirque below Cardiac Pass is then done on relatively safe terrain.

(2) The higher route follows the Mount Superior ridge from Cardiff Pass for about 0.7 mile to the rocky shoulder at the head of the avalanche slope marked in Fig. 6-23. The ridge is quite steep in spots, so some traversing back and forth is often necessary; the south side is usually safer for this purpose. From the shoulder, the route traverses north across the top of the avalanche slope just mentioned, then across a fairly steep gully to the cirque below Mount Superior and Cardiac Pass.

Three alternatives for climbing in the cirque are shown in Fig. 6-24. Cardiac Pass can be reached by approaching the cirque high from the left side, then traversing under the cliffs below the summit of Superior. (A touring party was involved in an avalanche here in February 1972.) One can also zig-zag directly

---

*The name of Cardiac Ridge was suggested by Charles Chauncey Hall, a prominent Salt Lake orthopedic corporation and active ski tourer, who observed that a person could have a heart attach just *looking* at this dangerous area.

†This route was first suggested by Dr. Ronald I. Perla, one of the leading avalanche authorities in North America, who spent several years at the now defunct Alta Avalanche Study Center.

Figure 6-23—Three routes are available from Cardiff Pass to Cardiac Pass, none of which is particularly safe. The bowl under Mount Superior is one of the most hazardous avalanche areas in the Wasatch.

up the middle of the cirque to the pass. (Another party was swept down in a slide there in December 1969.) A third alternative is to traverse to the pass from the right to avoid the

Figure 6-24—The ascent to Cardiac Ridge requires a crossing of this bowl. Any of the alternatives shown are advisable only with absolutely stable snow conditions.

north-facing slopes. (This has not been attempted with sufficient frequency to produce any reported avalanche incidents.) The climb from Alta to Cardiac Pass is 3.0 miles and, depending on the route, between 2300 and 2900 vertical feet.

The descent into Big Cottonwood Canyon has many possibilities, two of which are described here. They are labelled "upper" and "lower" in Fig. 6-25, which is a photo of Mill B South Fork. The two routes converge at Lake Blanche, which lies just below the Sundial massif, and separate again in the lower part of the canyon. Above the lake, the upper descent

Figure 6-25—Mill B South Fork has many touring possibilities. The route into Mineral Fork is shown in the photo, along with the infrequently skied area in the west branch of Mill B. The Sundial massif in the center of the photo is the emblem of the Wasatch Mountain Club.

route involves considerable avalanche hazard. It also requires much traversing and climbing, but the snow is sometimes better. The lower route to Lake Blanche also has some avalanche hazard, but the descent is smoother.

Below Lake Blanche the choice of routes depends largely on snow conditions. The lower route generally follows the hiking trail, which is quite narrow and steep in spots. It has the advantage, however, of offering good walking terrain if the snow ends before the tour (not an uncommon occurrence). The upper route crosses several hazardous areas, but the snow on the east-facing slopes is protected from the sun and often allows one to ski all the way to the bottom. The total length of Mill B South from Cardiac Pass is 4.9 miles with 4600 feet of elevation change.

MILL B SOUTH FORK FROM LOWER CARDIFF. In order to avoid (and also alleviate) the automobile congestion in Little Cottonwood Canyon, the Lake Blanche ski tour is often done from Big Cottonwood via Cardiff Fork. This alternative unfortunately involves a climb that is almost twice the distance and one and a half times the elevation gain as the standard approach from Alta. The tour basically follows the mining road up Mill D South to the Cardiff Mine complex. At this point a gradual traverse is taken to the right and up into the cirque below Cardiac Pass (Fig. 6-13). Routes and avalanche hazards in the upper reaches of Cardiff Fork have already been described. Total distance from the highway to the pass is 5.3 miles with an elevation gain of 3600 feet.

LAKE BLANCHE FROM THE "S"-CURVE. The third alternative for Mill B South avoids the avalanche hazards in upper Cardiff Fork. This tour starts at the bottom of the "S" curve in Big Cottonwood and follows the Forest Service road along the stream for about 0.3 miles and then the hiking trail up to Lake Blanche. Several possibilities are available from the lake. One can stay to the left and take the previously mentioned "lower" descent route to Cardiac Pass. A second option is to climb over the east ridge and ski into Mineral Fork, as described in the next section. Another alternative is to climb to the right of Sundial into the high valley bordered by the Dromedary and Sundial ridges; Fig. 6-25 shows that there is some delightful skiing terrain in this branch of Mill B South, but the only safe approach is from the bottom.

Upper Mineral Fork

For a ski tour that has only four miles of downhill, Mineral Fork has an unusually large number of possible approaches. The top of the canyon can be reached from Alta, from Cardiff Fork,

Figure 6-26—The two routes into upper Mineral Fork originate in Cardiff Fork and Mill B South Fork. The latter is very steep and hazardous in winter and spring.

from the "S" curve in Big Cottonwood Canyon, or by hiking up from the bottom as described in a previous section. All require exposure to hazardous terrain during both the climb and the descent. Two of the most straight-forward routes into upper Mineral are described here. Both are shown in Fig. 6-26, which is a photograph of the cirque.

The safest alternative that is marked in the figure avoids the big open bowl at the top and allows the tourer to ski on terrain that is somewhat protected from avalanches. The approach is from Cardiff Fork, so it can be reached from Alta or Big Cottonwood Canyon. Fig. 6-13 shows a moderately thick line of fir trees leading to the ridge from the top of Montreal Hill, which is just above the Cardiff Mine complex. The best ascent route is to climb through these trees and then up along the ridge another 100 yards to a favorable descent area. The run down to the jeep road in the bottom of Mineral Fork is the most challenging part of the tour. The canyon is quite flat below that except for the portion just above the Big Cottonwood highway. (See the earlier section on Lower Mineral Fork.) Total distance is 3500 feet over 3.9 miles.

The second possibility for upper Mineral should be attempted by only the most competent and knowledgeable ski tourers. It can be a superb powder run, but the avalanche hazard is extremely high. The route comes over the ridge from upper Mill B South at the southwest corner of the upper Mineral Fork cirque. Fig. 6-25 shows the approach. From Alta, one can go over Cardiac Pass, then traverse down and to the right for about 0.3 mile, staying as high as possible. The pass into Mineral is a small notch at 10,500 feet elevation. Skis may need to be removed for a short rock scramble in order to get there. Once over the ridge, however, there is almost always enough snow to ski right from the top. (It should be noted that a true glutton for punishment could get to this pass from the "S" curve by climbing about five miles and 4300 vertical feet along the Lake Blanche hiking trail.) Total descent into Mineral Fork is 3800 feet over 4.1 miles.

Broads Fork

Unlike most of the lower Big Cottonwood tours, the ascent into Broads Fork is almost always done from the bottom. Although a route exists between Mill B South (Lake Blanche) and Broads, it is an unusually risky venture that is rarely attempted. The only safe, sane, and practical alternative for the tourer in Broads Fork is the hiking trail that goes directly up the canyon and stops short of the upper avalanche-prone cirque beneath the summits of Dromedary, Sunrise, and Twin Peaks.

The hiking trail into Broads Fork starts at the lower end of the "S" curve, just across the bridge from the Big Cottonwood highway. It traverses westerly and upward for about 0.4 mile to the top of a secondary ridge overlooking the highway below. From this point the trail bends to the south and crosses the stream after another 0.5 mile. For the next 1.2 miles, any of several minor, tree-covered ridges (actually glacial morraines) can be followed to a prominent knoll that serves as an excellent viewpoint for the Broads Fork bowl. Because of severe avalance hazard in the cirque, the tour should end at this point. Total climb is 2100 feet over 2.1 miles.

Figure 6-27—The view from the bottom of the upper cirque in Broads Fork is spectacular. It is not advisable to climb any further.

Fig. 6-27 shows the spectacular avalanche terrain in upper Broads Fork. It is important for the skier to enjoy this outstanding alpine scenery because it is certainly the high point of the tour. The descent, like that of the hiking trail below Lake Blanche, will undoubtedly make him wish that he had brought along snowshoes (or stayed at home)! It is not advisable to

Figure 6-28—For obvious reasons, Stairs Gulch is not a good place to be in winter or spring.

abandon the trail in favor of skiing the lower portion of Broads. Just above the Big Cottonwood stream there is a very steep slope covered with thickets of nearly impenetrable brush.

Stairs Gulch

Stairs Gulch is *almost* never entered in winter. The Forest Service and other knowledgeable agencies wish that it be *absolutely* never entered in either winter or spring. Stairs Gulch is a very narrow, winding canyon that goes about 2.0 miles from the Big Cottonwood highway to its crest at the ridge below Twin Peaks. In that distance, the canyon rises 4600 vertical feet, which means that it has an average slope of almost 30°. (The canyon is actually much steeper near the top.) The upper part of Stairs Gulch is an immense rock slab which frequently sends powerful avalanches into the main gully below. The Big Cottonwood highway has been buried to depths of 40 feet or more. The photograph of the canyon (Fig. 6-28) illustrates why the area is not recommended for ski touring. □

7 LITTLE COTTONWOOD CANYON

Little Cottonwood Canyon has had a turbulent and controversial history for over a century. Until the miners came looking for gold and silver, the canyon was used primarily as a source of granite for the Salt Lake Temple and lumber for buildings in the valley. Alta had only a steam sawmill and a boarding house in 1868, but five years later its population had grown to about 8,000! In the 1870's, more than 100 men were killed in barroom disputes.

By 1880 most of the timber had been cut off the slopes around Alta by the miners. This left the area particularly susceptible to avalanches from the surrounding mountainsides. "SIX POOR SOULS HURLED INTO ETERNITY" reads the headline of the January 15, 1881, issue of *The Daily Tribune*. The article describes a "fearful" avalanche that "swept from the Davenport Divide" crushing the Grizzly Boarding House. In the five day period of January 12 to 17, 1881, fifteen lives were lost by snow slides in Little Cottonwood and American Fork Canyons. On March 11, 1884, under a headline "DEATH IN A SNOWSLIDE", the *Tribune* again describes Alta's visitation by a "Horribly Destructive Avalanche" leaving "Ten Men And Two Women Killed And Terribly Mangled":

163

"It is as though the hand of God had swept quickly over the earth, and with no noise, confusion, or notice, had quietly blotted out of existence so many lives and so much property, as a man would snuff out a candle...

The slide was the most fearful and destructive that has ever visited Alta. It started from the summit of the Equitable Gulch and with the rapidity of a flash made its way to the Rattler Ravine above Grizzly Flat. Continuing downwards it struck and carried away the New Emma boiler house, blacksmith shop, boarding house, and concentrating works, instantly killing twelve persons who had sought the place for safety."

Just a year later, on February 14, 1885, "The Worst Disaster Yet To Befall That Snowy Region" occurred, killing sixteen persons and destroying a good portion of Emmaville, a small cluster of businesses and residences just a short distance below the city of Alta.*

Although recent history seems dull by comparison, Little Cottonwood has stayed in the news. Because it provides a significant percentage of the culinary water consumed in Salt Lake County, great opposition has been raised to further incursions by ski area developers and condominium builders who are active in the canyon. Also in this decade there has been an effort to preserve in its present condition much of the land between Little Cottonwood and American Fork Canyons by setting up the Lone Peak Wilderness Area. Forest Service and Congressional figures have vascillated so frequently on this issue.that its future is presently in some doubt. And of course the perennial avalanches generate even more headlines for the canyon.

Just as Little Cottonwood is rich in lore and history, it also has an abundance of ski touring possibilities. Of all the canyons in the Wasatch, this one provides access to the largest quantity and variety of ski touring terrain. But the threat of avalanche hangs as heavily above the skier of today as it once hung over the miners of yesteryear. The hillsides show little sign of returning to their former forested state, even after 100 years. The fragile canyon ecology continues to suffer from man's greed.

For the beginner skier there are the gentle slopes of Albion Basin which was described in Chapter 3. For those whose touring

---

*Because many of these same slide paths threaten current lodges, homes, ski and parking areas, the U.S. Forest Service avalanche control teams fire several thousand rounds of artillery every winter in an effort to knock the snow down before depths build up to catastrophic size. Even with such extensive procedures, unplanned slides sometimes release, causing property damage and injuries.

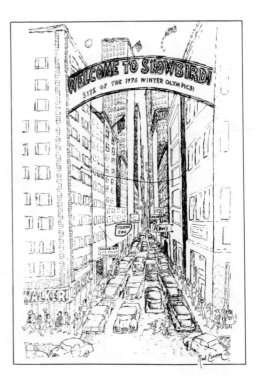

Figure 7-1—Culminating over 100 years of turmoil in Little Cottonwood Canyon was the proposal to make it a site for the 1976 Winter Olympics. The *Daily Utah Chronicle* satirized the situation with this cartoon.

abilities are more intermediate, there are several routes in the Alta area, including Catherine Pass, Grizzly Gulch, and Cardiff Pass. Further down the canyon, below the concrete reminders of man's "progress", are White Pine and Red Pine. The advanced skier will enjoy Maybird and Hogum Forks, with the Pfeifferhorn and other nearby summits serving as mountaineering variety for those seeking such a diversion.

Little Cottonwood Canyon is also the starting point for a number of trans-canyon tours into Big Cottonwood Canyon, American Fork Canyon, Bells Canyon, or the Dry Creek drainage above the community of Alpine. Tours into Big Cottonwood have been described in Chapter 6. American Fork Canyon tours and those into Alpine will be described in Chapter 8. Bells Canyon tours are included in this chapter.

This chapter treats the Little Cottonwood Canyon tours in what the authors believe to be the order of increasing difficulty. Remember, though, that the "intermediate", "advanced", and "super" categories have been introduced after considerable bureaucratic arbitration. One man's "advanced" tour is, after all, another's "intermediate"!

165

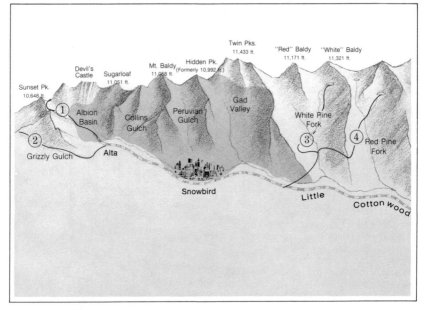

Figure 7-2—The intermediate tours described in this chapter are (1) Albion Basin, (2) Grizzly Gulch, (3) White Pine, and (4) Red Pine Canyon. Not shown on the map is the route to Cardiff Pass.

INTERMEDIATE TOURS

Catherine Pass/Albion Hut

CATHERINE PASS.   One of the easiest intermediate outings in the Wasatch is an extension of the Albion Basin tour described in Chapter 3. Catherine Pass is on the east ridge of Albion Basin overlooking Brighton, and Albion Hut is about 0.5 mile south of the pass along the same ridge. The most popular hiking and touring route between Alta and Brighton is over Catherine Pass. (The tour from Brighton to the pass was described in Chapter 6).

Access to Albion Basin is basically along the Forest Service Road which is a continuation of the Little Cottonwood Canyon highway. It is plowed only to the base of the ski lifts, so the tour begins at the end of the parking lot. To get to Catherine Pass it is best to follow the road only until it passes under the Albion

166

ski lift, then to bear left and follow the ski trail to the top of the chair lift. From there, a gradual traverse up and to the left takes the skier into the drainage that leads eastward to Catherine Pass.

The climb is quite gentle for about half a mile, followed by a large flat meadow and a short steeper section just below the pass. The south slope of Mt. Tuscarora, which rises sharply on the left side of the touring route, should be avoided if the avalanche situation is at all hazardous. Total elevation gain from the parking lot to Catherine Pass is about 1400 feet over three miles.

ALBION HUT. The Albion hut is nestled so snugly in a stand of fir trees that it is often difficult to find in the winter. It is a metal Quonset hut left over from World War II with a tall "Santa Claus chimney" for entry in the snowy months when the front door is buried. The structure was built in the late 40's by the Salt Lake County Recreation Department as part of a program to establish shelters for hikers and tourers. Similar buildings were also constructed at Snake Creek Pass and Germania Pass, but both are gone now. Although the Albion hut is not carefully maintained, its location away from popular trails has slowed its deterioration.

To get to the hut, simply follow the ridge south from Catherine Pass. About halfway to Sunset Peak the ridge splits, with one branch going to the left around Lake Catherine and our route to the right around Albion Basin. The first high spot on the right branch is called Point Supreme,[†] which is about 400 vertical feet above the pass. Beyond this peak is a saddle and then a dense clump of fir trees which hides the Albion Hut. The interior of the structure is quite gloomy in winter, but it provides a shelter with all the comforts of home (tables, benches, stove) for people needing to get out of the weather. Anyone using the hut is encouraged to leave it as clean and pleasant as possible for others.

Several possibilities exist for the descent back into Albion Basin. The easiest is to retrace the route of ascent that was just described. Another good alternative is to proceed along the ridge toward Devil's Castle and ski the southern slopes of Albion Basin (an area, incidently, where Alta plans to build yet another ski lift). This route has plenty of open slopes with lots of room for maneuvering in the deep snow. (Fig. 7-3.) A third way down

---

† Point Supreme is unfortunately a popular landing spot for helicopter skiers.

Labels in image: Mt. Wolverine, Catherine Pass, Albion Hut, Ski Lift, Ski Lift, Albion Basin

Figure 7-3—Albion Basin lies at the head of Little Cottonwood Canyon. From its upper ridge a tourer can ski into Big Cottonwood or American Fork Canyons, as well as the town of Midway to the east.

from the hut is the ridge that goes into the basin from Point Supreme. This can be a good run if the helicopter "Johns" haven't wasted all the powder. The terrain is more difficult in this area, and caution is needed near the bottom to avoid cliffs and steep gullies.

Grizzly Gulch/Twin Lakes Pass

Grizzly Gulch was the scene of some of Alta's most intense mining activity in the late nineteenth and early twentieth centuries. The Michigan-Utah Mines continued to send ore down the canyon long after most others had been deserted by

Figure 7-4—Grizzly Gulch starts at Alta and leads to Twin Lakes Pass which overlooks the Brighton ski area. It can also be approached from the Forest Service Guard Station via the mining road along the left side of the photo.

their disillusioned owners. In 1904, some of the Michigan-Utah's predecessors undertook one of the most monumental engineering feats in local mining history. They built an aerial tramway to carry ore from Michigan City (about half way up Grizzly Gulch) down to Tanner's Flat, a distance of about 4.5 miles. The tram carried thousands of tons of valuable cargo before it creaked to a halt in 1923. Some of the old wooden towers are still visible in Grizzly Gulch, but many were torn down and used for the first Collins ski lift at Alta in 1938.

There are two ways into Grizzly Gulch from Alta. The direct route starts on the north side of the upper parking lot near the end of the plowed highway. The tour follows a narrow gully for about 0.8 mile until it widens into a broad flat area. This used to be the site of Michigan City. From there, you can follow the power line directly east all the way to Twin Lakes Pass, which overlooks the Brighton ski area. Total climb is 1.3 miles and 1200 vertical feet.

The second route is longer (1.9 miles and 1350 vertical feet), but it is more gradual and avoids the gully at the bottom. It starts at the Forest Service Guard Station at the west end of town and follows a jeep road that parallels the highway and eventually intersects the first route near Michigan City Flat. This is a scenic tour on gentle terrain, but there can be great avalanche danger from above during and after a storm. Both routes can be seen in the photograph in Fig. 7-4.

There are several popular routes of descent. One possibility is to cross over into Brighton and return via Catherine Pass. (See Chapter 6.) Another is to follow the ridge to Mount Wolverine and take one of several routes from there. (This tour is also described in Chapter 6.) The most obvious alternative is simply to retrace the ascent route in its entirety. A final option is to climb along the Mount Wolverine ridge to a small prominence about half way to the summit. From that point you can ski down the ridge which forms the south boundary of Grizzly Gulch, eventually ending at the parking lot where the tour began.

Cardiff Pass

A description of the Alta-oriented ski tours would be incomplete without mentioning Cardiff Pass. It's importance to serious tourers is paramount. This pass is the starting point for several superb Big Cottonwood trips, such as Cardiff Fork, Mineral Fork and the popular Lake Blanche tour. Many people like to climb to the pass just to enjoy the view and then ski back down to Alta, although the south-facing snow is often not very good.

Some of the early miners reportedly used a different method of transportation to town from their workings high up on the hillsides near Cardiff Pass. The *Alta Independent* described one such descent in 1873.

"This morning, the snow being very hard, a man mounted his steed, a large shovel, and started to come down to the city. He came at the rate of 50 miles per hour for about 2,000 feet when he found it impossible to keep his seat, and each was trying to beat the other to town. The shovel came on as gracefully as the soaring of an eagle; while the movements of the man resembled the gracefulness of a baby elephant; the acts he went through would make the most perfect acrobat feel the blush of shame in a professional line. He landed at the foot of the mountain unhurt, but considerably paled from exertion of the race."

This could be a prophetic description of the nordic skier's first attempts on a steep slope.

The ascent to Cardiff Pass starts at the U.S. Forest Service Guard Station west of town. (See Fig. 6-12.) The first step is to climb past the buildings and above the gun tower. (A jeep road can be followed in this area.) Next, traverse upward in a northwesterly direction until the power line is intercepted. This power line should be followed all the way to the pass since it stays on a relatively avalanche-free secondary ridge. Many tourers erroneously steer for the open slopes west of the wires, thus exposing themselves to the serious avalanche threat illustrated in Fig. 2-13. Total distance to Cardiff Pass is about a mile with a 1400 foot elevation gain.

White Pine Lake

White Pine has been a canyon of many uses. At one time it was a major source of Engleman spruce, from which it gained its name. These trees were used for decades by miners in Little Cottonwood Canyon and builders in the valley. Later a jeep road and a dam were built as part of the Salt Lake water storage program. It has been an important part of our water system ever since. In 1959 this canyon was the scene of one of the largest and most destructive avalanches to occur in the Wasatch Mountains for many years. The remains can still be observed. Tree stumps 10 feet high and 3 feet in diameter stand as grim reminders of the incredible power generated by a wave of moving snow.

White Pine has recently become the most controversial canyon in the Wasatch. The debate is centered over whether it should be included in a Lone Peak Wilderness Area or the Snow-

Figure 7-5—White Pine Canyon is known for its terribly destructive avalanche paths, some of which have denuded hillsides and splintered trees as large as three feet in diameter.

bird ski area.* If the developers are successful in getting White Pine, a superb touring spot will be lost, and cross country skiers will be effectively locked out of *more than half* of the skiable terrain in Little Cottonwood Canyon. Will the Californians win again?

Most of White Pine is delightful intermediate touring terrain. Except for the lower 800 feet of elevation and the upper cirques, the canyon is not at all steep. The easiest route to the lake follows a jeep road all the way from the bottom. The tour is usually started just above the Little Pine Slide Area on the highway. (Be careful not to park between the signs.) A small bridge† crosses Little Cottonwood Creek east of White Pine Canyon, and the jeep road climbs gently westward from there. About 0.9 mile from the highway, the road bends sharply to the

---

*It has been estimated that if White Pine becomes part of the Snowbird ski area, demolition teams will have to double the number of explosive missiles used to control their slopes, bringing the total to more than 4,000 rounds of ammunition per year.

†Finding this bridge in winter can be the most difficult part of the tour. A summer reconnaissance is worthwhile.

Figure 7-6—White Pine is one of the most popular intermediate touring areas in Little Cottonwood. Its upper bowls, which can be reached from American Fork Canyon (East Pass and West Pass), have some extremely challenging and hazardous terrain.

left. (The Red Pine hiking trail starts here and goes to the right across the stream.) The road switches back and forth and then levels off for the next 1.2 miles. The jeep road stays on the left side of the canyon and passes several large avalanche runout zones as shown in Fig. 7-6. After reaching the lake, note that it is surrounded by slide paths that should always be avoided. The total climb is 2400 feet over 3.0 miles.

An alternate route that avoids some of the potentially dangerous areas stays in the more wooded areas in the center of the canyon, away from the slide paths. Either of these routes is a good way to return to the highway.

Red Pine Lake

Red Pine Canyon, like its easterly neighbor, has excellent intermediate terrain below the upper cirque, but the top 800 feet should be saved for the experts. The lower lake, with its exquisite alpine setting, is a popular destination for hikers in the summertime and tourers in the winter.

The Red Pine Lake ski tour commences at the same place as the White Pine trip. The route proceeds across the bridge and along the jeep road for 0.9 mile. The easiest way into Red Pine is to bear right and cross the stream where the White Pine road bends sharply to the left. A trail traverses from there around the White Pine-Red Pine ridge. From a small plateau on the ridge, the trail angles to the south along the steep, west-facing (and avalanche-prone) slopes of Red Pine Canyon. For the next 1.3 miles the trail stays on the west side, high above the stream bed. After climbing through a grove of aspens, the touring route intersects the stream near a large mine dump. There is usually drinking water here, so it's a good lunch stop.

From the mine dump there are two excellent routes to lower Red Pine Lake. The first one continues directly south along the open slopes on the east side of the canyon. The other route drifts to the right and climbs through Douglas Fir trees (after which the canyon was named). The possibilities are obvious in Fig. 7-7. Little Cottonwood Canyon highway to Red Pine Lake is 3.1 miles with 2000 feet of elevation gain.

Several possibilities are available to the tourer at Red Pine Lake. Anyone wanting more height can climb through the trees above the lake that are visible in the photo. (The avalanche path west of the trees should be avoided at all costs.) An ascent of only 400 feet gets the tourer to upper Red Pine Lake. Anything beyond that is not recommended. The descent back to the lower lake should also be in the protection of the trees.

At least three alternatives exist for returning to the highway. The simplest is to retrace the upward track all the way to the car. If you want powder skiing, however, the west side of the canyon is often better. Simply traverse to the left from the lake, without losing too much elevation, until you find a good spot to go down through the trees. There are places all along the canyon where an intermediate skier can get to the stream, but some areas are quite steep and heavily wooded. Be careful not to go

White Baldy

(to Dry Creek)

Upper Lakes

Red Pine Lake

Mine

Red Pine Canyon

Figure 7-7—Red Pine Canyon provides access for many advanced and super tours, including Maybird, Hogum, Coalpit, Bells, Dry Creek, and American Fork. It is also a popular intermediate skiing area in its own right. Fig. 7-9 shows the routes into other canyons.

too far on the west side, however, or there will be a long climb back to the White Pine trail.

The final descent route to be described here is the ridge between Red Pine and Maybird. The upper section has very

175

large, widely-spaced fir trees and is delightful skiing terrain. About a third of the way down to the highway, it is best to bear right and ski on the east-facing slopes near the ridge. The lower end of the ridge is extremely steep, so one should ski along the stream. The tour isn't over at Little Cottonwood Creek. There is no bridge, so getting across can be interesting, to say the least. After the crossing, there is a short climb to the highway and you can walk or hitchhike back to the starting point. (A car can't be parked at the bottom of Red Pine because it's across from the Tanners Gulch avalanche area.) Descent from the lower lake is 2400 feet over 2.4 miles.

ADVANCED TOURS

Little Cottonwood Canyon has a great deal of very difficult skiing terrain, all the way from Alta to Bell's Canyon. The high cirques in all the side canyons are extremely steep with very little vegetation to hold the snow in place. Touring in these areas should only be done with great caution. It is usually best to save these tours until late in the winter after the cold, snowy season has passed.

The canyons west of Red Pine are much less heavily used than the areas already described in this chapter. Most of them show little effect of man's presence, and for good reason. Their accessibility, slope, complexity of terrain, and avalanche hazard require more stamina, knowledge, and skiing ability than the others. The lower sections are steep, narrow gullies, so they must be entered from the top. This can involve a long hike. To get to upper Hogum Fork, for example, one must start at the bottom of White Pine, traverse up and across Red Pine and Maybird, and then climb into Hogum.

Although there are many tours in Little Cottonwood that require advanced skiing ability, only four are described in this section. They are Maybird Gulch, Hogum Fork, Pfeifferhorn Peak, and Upper White Pine. Others which involve a much longer hike and more hazard are classified as "super tours" and are treated later.

Maybird Gulch

Upper Maybird is one of the most scenic areas in the Wasatch, with the spectacular Pfeifferhorn massif rising at its head. This is certainly an ideal spot for sunshine and camera. In fact, the climb into Maybird from Red Pine is easy enough

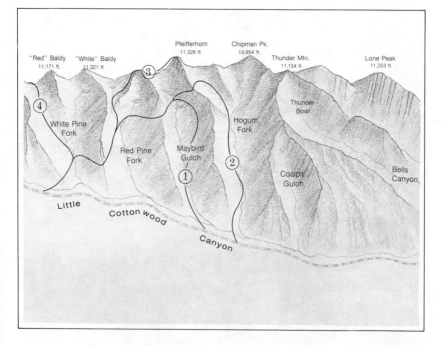

Figure 7-8—Only four Little Cottonwood tours have been classified as advanced: (1) Maybird Gulch, (2) Hogum Fork, (3) the Pfeifferhorn and (4) Alta to White Pine.

for an intermediate tourer to ski over for picture taking and then return the same way.

There are two popular ways into Maybird. One possibility is to start climbing the west side of Red Pine Canyon from the mine dump described in the Red Pine Lake section (See Fig. 7-9.) From the top of the first steep pitch, simply traverse up through the firs into the Maybird drainage. The second route is from lower Red Pine Lake. Ski down and to the left around the Red Pine-Maybird ridge below the steep open slopes shown in the photo. Once into the canyon, a short climb through wooded terrain takes the tourer to a view that is worth the effort. The distance from lower White Pine is 3.9 miles with 2200 feet of elevation gain.

The upper cirque of Maybird Gulch offers two options for the descent. The first is to ski directly down the main streambed. Most of the run into Little Cottonwood Canyon is in a deep ravine, bordered on both sides by extremely steep slopes. This gully is not a good place to be when avalanche conditions are a concern. Another potential danger along the streambed is holes

177

Figure 7-9—The Pfeifferhorn rises dramatically at the head of the ridge between Maybird and Hogum Forks. The route over that ridge is shown in the photo, along with the route from Red Pine Lake to the east ridge of the Pfeifferhorn.

in the snow which are sometimes created by the water flowing underneath. The descent is 3000 feet over 2.5 miles.

The second possibility for the descent into Maybird involves traversing high into the western reaches of the canyon, as shown in Fig. 7-9 and 7-10. The broad open slope directly below the Maybird-Hogum ridge can be skied for nearly the entire length of the gulch. This slope is relatively safe, but it is exposed to the wind and may not prove to be enticing to the powder connoisseur. At the end of this area, it becomes necessary to drop into the main Maybird ravine. This is accomplished by descending through the trees in a steep, narrow couloir (which can be difficult to locate for someone not familiar with the terrain).

There is no bridge over Little Cottonwood Creek at the bottom of Maybird, so the crossing can prove to be interesting. (This is another good place for a camera.) If you planned ahead

Figure 7-10—The lower part of Maybird Gulch is a narrow gully with steep wooded sides.

and left a car, the tour is completed with a short climb from the creek to the highway.

Hogum Fork

Hogum Fork, one of the largest drainages in Little Cottonwood Canyon, has three upper cirques, headed by the Pfeifferhorn, Chipman Peak and Thunder Mountain. Like Maybird, it

Figure 7-11—Hogum Fork is the largest side canyon in Little Cottonwood. It is seldom visited by ski tourers.

is open at the top with a steep narrow gully at the lower end. The difference is in magnitude. Hogum has much more area, is less accessible, has greater avalanche hazard, and is much steeper and trickier to negotiate at the bottom. It doesn't even appear to be skiable from the road.

The basic climbing route starts the same as that into Maybird (White Pine to Red Pine to Maybird). Just below the summit of Pfeifferhorn, there is a pass in the Maybird-Hogum Ridge that can be reached by zig-zagging up from the Maybird side. Caution is urged in this area, it should not be attempted unless the snow is stable. The distance from the bottom of White Pine to the Hogum Ridge is 4.4 miles and 2700 feet.

The open terrain in upper Hogum always looks inviting (Fig. 7-11), but this broad treeless expanse is very exposed to

Figure 7-12 — Lower Hogum is steep, narrow, brushy and rocky. With luck, you can find a route down to the stream. The circled building is an abandoned mill.

wind and sun. The skiing may vary from delightful powder turns through open cirques and scattered trees, to flailing through breakable crust and wind-packed snow. Whatever delights are found in upper Hogum, they are invariably replaced by agonizing struggles in the lower section. The steep rocky terrain is very brushy in places and to make matters worse, the snow at the bottom is often marginal due to its low elevation. The crossing of Little Cottonwood Creek can also be traumatic since there is no bridge. The descent is 3800 feet over 3.4 miles.

To anyone undertaking this tour, we recommend a careful examination of Fig. 7-12 to choose a route down the lower sec-

181

tion. Good luck!

Pfeifferhorn Peak

A winter ascent of Pfeifferhorn is really more of a mountaineering outing than a ski tour. We include it in this book only because it is such a popular trip. Despite its many spectacular rocky faces and steep snowy couloirs, the peak can be climbed by a strong tourer with a good guide, even if one has only limited mountaineering experience.

From upper Red Pine Lake there are two routes commonly used to reach the 11,326 foot summit of the Pfeifferhorn. The most direct and most frequently attempted approach is along the east ridge. Less common, but easier and safer, is the west ridge. These routes are labeled (1) and (2), respectively, in Fig. 7-13. Both alternatives require an ascent of the upper Red Pine Ridge. This is an extremely exposed area, as shown in Fig. 7-9, and great caution must be exercised. The usual route is to climb the prominent secondary ridge that starts just below the upper lake. There are hazardous avalanche paths on each side of this ridge, so it is imperative to stay as close as possible to its crest. It may be necessary to remove your skis in order to negotiate the last few feet to the top.

ROUTE 1. The direct route to the Pfeifferhorn is along the east ridge as illustrated in Fig. 7-13. Skis are usually removed before attempting the last part of the ridge and the final climb to the summit. Portions of the crest are narrow and rocky, and can cause some difficulties for a skier. Directly below the summit massif, there is a steep hanging snowfield. This is an obvious avalanche area and should be skirted along the right flank close to the ridge overlooking Maybird Gulch. Total climb from the bottom of White Pine is 3700 feet and 5.3 miles.

ROUTE 2. The second alternative is for the tourer who is uncertain of the hanging summit snowfield. This route drops down into Dry Creek Canyon, which borders the Pfeifferhorn to the south, and makes a wide loop around the base of the peak. The south facing slopes that must be crossed usually stabilize as quickly as any, but there is still much exposure from above. Skis should be removed at the ridge overlooking Hogum Fork. The final ascent to the summit is along the west ridge, which is not quite as steep and dangerous as the previously described route. The distance for this climb is 6.0 miles.

Figure 7-13—Most winter ascents of the Pfeifferhorn are done via (1) the east or (2) the west ridge. The latter route is longer, but it is safer and requires less mountaineering skill.

The obvious way down after an assault on the Pfeifferhorn is to retrace the route followed on the way up. This means skiing (or walking) down into Red Pine, which is certainly not the most secure place to spend an afternoon. An alternative is to go down the Dry Creek drainage to the town of Alpine. The snow on the south-facing slopes is often less than spectacular, snow-mobiles may be encountered at lower elevations, and the car shuttle is horrendous, but at least it's safe. More discussion of Dry Creek is found in Chapter 8.

Upper White Pine (From Alta)

The final advanced tour to be described in this chapter is Upper White Pine Canyon. It is obvious from Fig. 7-6 that this is an extremely hazardous area with avalanche paths coming into the cirques from all sides.

The canyon has two branches separated by a rocky summit known as Red Baldy. American Fork Twin Peaks are at the top of the White Pine-Gad Valley Ridge and White Baldy is between White Pine and Red Pine. At the head of each branch is a pass leading to American Fork Canyon. For convenience, they are labeled "East Pass" and "West Pass' in the photo.

183

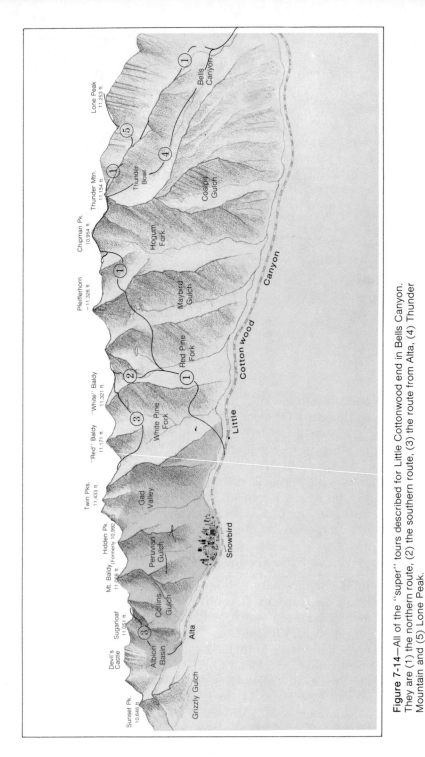

Figure 7-14—All of the "super" tours described for Little Cottonwood end in Bells Canyon. They are (1) the northern route, (2) the southern route, (3) the route from Alta, (4) Thunder Mountain and (5) Lone Peak.

It makes little sense to approach either pass from the White Pine side of the ridge. A tourer would have to expose himself to severe avalanche danger for much too long a time. Safer routes exist on the American Fork side and are accessible from Alta. Details of these tours are found in Chapter 8.

A tourer who ventures into White Pine Canyon from the top is well-advised not to linger on the headwall in the upper cirque. Only expert fall-line skiers should attempt a descent as steep as this. It is not an area for long traverses. The run to Little Cottonwood Creek from East Pass is 3100 feet over 3.5 miles.

SUPER TOURS

It has been suggested that a touch of "lunacy" is necessary in order to undertake one of the Little Cottonwood "super tours". While the need for lunacy may be debatable, the need for moonlight is a near certainty for these epic journeys. In addition, the tourer should be intimately familiar with the terrain in both winter and summer, be in top physical condition, be an expert avalanche analyst and be prepared for any emergency (including an overnight stay). The tours are best done in late winter when the days are long and the snow is most stable.

The routes are not described in great detail in this section. It is assumed that anyone attempting one of these tours will need only a rough outline. They are marked on the map in Fig. 7-14.

Bells Canyon

Bells Canyon, reportedly the site of Porter Rockwell's long lost gold mine, is a glacial canyon that empties into the Salt Lake Valley just south of Little Cottonwood. Although it is not part of Little Cottonwood Canyon, much of the ski touring approach route takes place there, necessitating its inclusion in this chapter. Bells starts at an elevation of 5100 feet just east of the community of Granite. It provides culinary and irrigation water to thousands of people in the area. Access to the canyon is controlled by a private water company, so permission should be obtained before skiing there.

Fig. 7-15 is a photograph of Bells Canyon. It is about 6.3 miles in length and terminates in two large branches. Lone Peak (elevation 11,253 feet) and Thunder Mountain (11,154 feet) are at the heads of the two branches. Thus, a descent (or ascent)

Figure 7-15—Bells Canyon has two very large glacial cirques. Route (1) stays in the west branch near the Lone Peak massif. Routes (2) and (3) go into Thunder Bowl from the summit of Thunder Mountain.

could be more than 6,000 vertical feet. It is not uncommon for the lower 1500 feet to have poor snow cover and nearly impenetrable brush, but the upper cirques can be delightful.

A ski tour into Bells is usually started from the bottom of White Pine Canyon, although it has been done from Alta. All of the routes generally follow the ridge between Little Cottonwood and Dry Creek to the top of Bells Canyon, with side trips possible to Lone Peak and Thunder Mountain. The five alternatives described in this text are shown in Fig. 7-14. The routes are outlined in the following sections.

STANDARD ROUTE — NORTHERN VARIATION. The standard Bells Canyon tour is done by one of two very distinct routes. The first to be described goes north of the Pfeifferhorn, and the other goes to the south. The northern route is the more common and the shorter of the two, but it has more exposure to avalanche hazard in upper Hogum Fork.

Figure 7-16—Upper Hogum Fork is used for access to Bells Canyon. The northern route (A) crosses the entire Fork from the Maybird ridge. The southern route (B) has only a short section in Hogum. The peak of Thunder Mountain is reached by (C). Two photos of the area are included for better perspective.

Starting from the Little Cottonwood highway, the northern route follows the White Pine/Red Pine Lake trail and crosses into the upper part of Maybird Gulch (Fig. 7-9). It next goes over the Maybird/Hogum divide and traverses upward around the rocky buttress that separates the east and center cirques of Hogum. This route is labeled "A" in Fig. 7-16. It continues to

187

climb toward the steep headwall just west of the saddle in the center cirque. The ascent of this headwall is one of the most hazardous parts of the tour.

From the top of Hogum Fork, ski south for several hundred yards to the gentle saddle between the main ridge and Chipman Peak. Congratulations, the worst is now over! The remainder of the trip to Bells Canyon is a northwesterly traverse with very little elevation change. Do not be tempted to drop any lower or you will end up in some steep and time-consuming terrain in the Lake Hardy drainage. This route is 6.6 miles with more than 3000 feet of climbing.

The top of Bells is a good spot for a scenic lunch stop (or dinner if your pace is particularly slow). The most common descent route is labeled (1) in Fig. 7-15. It stays in the open slopes below the rocky walls of Lone Peak. In the lower part of the canyon, the greatest challenge is to avoid thick brush and minimize the bushwacking. The left side of Bells provides a relatively open route most of the way, but the bottom is usually less than ideal. The descent from the pass is 6.3 miles with 5300 feet of vertical.

STANDARD ROUTE – SOUTHERN VERSION. The southern route to Bells Canyon is the same as the northern approach except for a section of about 2.5 miles between Red Pine Lake and Chipman Peak. From the bottom of White Pine, it climbs to Upper Red Pine Lake and then to the ridge (Fig. 7-9). Next, it drops into the Dry Creek Drainage and traverses west for about 1.5 miles below the Pfeifferhorn and below the next peak to the west. If a relatively constant elevation is maintained, the traverse will end at the pass to the middle cirque of Hogum Fork. From this saddle, the route drops a short distance into Hogum and joins the northern route for the steep climb toward Chipman Peak. (See "B" in Fig. 7-16.) The remainder of the tour is the same as previously described. This route is 7.3 miles to the top of Bells.

BELLS CANYON FROM ALTA. The most notorious super tour is the trip from Alta to Bells Canyon.* A particularly early start is in order to avoid darkness in lower Bells. The route goes over the pass at the top of the Sugarloaf lift at Alta and ascends to the summit of American Fork Twin Peaks. It then drops into upper White Pine Canyon. (A complete description of the Alta to White Pine tour is in the next chapter.) The most direct route

---

*This route was first completed by A. Kelner and B. Christenson in May 1969. The tour started at 2:00 a.m. and ended 19 hours later in Granite. An interesting sidelight of this trip was that it was done with downhill skis, but no climbing skins were used!

188

across White Pine is to drop down to the lake and then climb the steep couloir on the west side of the bowl to the White Pine/ Red Pine ridge. Next traverse the upper Red Pine cirque and intersect the southern route at the Dry Creek divide. The trip from Alta to the bottom of Bells is about 17 miles long. This is truly a super tour!

Thunder Mountain

It is a simple matter to climb to the summit of Thunder Mountain from the Bells Canyon divide. Simply follow the ridge for 0.7 mile. Some side-stepping or rock-scrambling may be required, but there is only about 700 feet of elevation change.

An alternative approach to Thunder is much shorter and less complicated than the standard route, but it may be very hazardous. The route is labeled "C" in Fig. 7-16. It follows a series of steep bowls in upper Hogum Fork and ascends directly to the summit via Hogum's west cirque. This approach is only 6.5 miles long.

Two routes will be described from Thunder Mountain into Bells Canyon. Both start with a descent of the beautiful bowl that is so evident from downtown Salt Lake City. Many people have undoubtedly wished for a tram to the top of this peak. Unfortunately, the upper bowl is quite short, and considerable skill in route finding and avalanche avoidance is necessary to get into the main Bells drainage. The route marked "2" in Fig. 7-15 is the most reliable. A long upward traverse is required below the bowl, but the terrain is quite good. Route "3" looks the most inviting in the photograph, but there are several cliff bands that require considerable snow depth in order for a skier to go down.

Lone Peak

If the standard Bells Canyon tour doesn't provide enough exercise and excitement for the mountaineering ski tourer, an additional climb of 800 vertical feet will take him to the peak, after which the proposed Lone Peak Wilderness Area was named. This is an extremely difficult and hazardous undertaking, so extreme caution is advised. A steep couloir, that is usually very wind-blown must be ascended, so a rope and ice axe are in order. The hike along the ridge to the summit is very exposed, so the rope will probably be needed there also.† □

---

† Lone Peak can also be climbed in winter by following the normal summer hiking route up the west ridge from Draper.

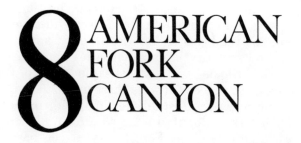

8 AMERICAN FORK CANYON

American Fork is the largest canyon to be described in this book. It contains thousands of acres of extremely challenging skiing, much of which is on west and south facing slopes. There is also a great deal of intermediate terrain in the bottom of the drainage for the more conservative tourer. It is unfortunately a long drive from either Salt Lake or Provo, particularly if you want to start an outing at Alta and ski down the canyon.

The history of American Fork Canyon is quite intriguing. Its chronology follows that of others in the Wasatch Mountains, but this canyon has suffered more than most from the activities of man over the last century. The interesting thing about American Fork history is that it involves not only mistreatment and degradation, but also some attempts at reclamation and restoration. A summary is included here in hopes of engendering a deeper awareness and concern for the local canyons, which are valuable for more than just recreation.

From the very beginning, the only people who did not cause irreparable damage to this canyon were its original inhabitants (the Indians) and the early pioneers who emigrated from the East. They had one thing in common-a simple life requiring little for survival. The mountains were vital to their existance, providing necessary water and timber. As Mormon communities grew, greater demands were placed on the resources of nearby canyons, but under Brigham Young's guidance, this priceless asset was protected.

Before too many years, the "Eastern establishment" became suspicious of the "Mormon establishment" and their unusual ways. The federal government considered various possibilities for handling this growing concern. It was finally decided to send an Army detachment to Utah to detumefy the situation. One of their strategies was to utilize the mining potential of the local canyons. It was hoped that members of the Army could prospect for and discover deposits of minerals. The area would then be attractive to "gentile" miners who would come here in great numbers and dilute the influence of the Latter Day Saints.*

During the 1860's, men from Johnston's Army discovered silver, lead, and gold at the head of American Fork Canyon. It was not until 1871, however, that mining activities were started in earnest. This marked the beginning of the exploitation of this once-beautiful canyon. So successful were these initial ventures, that two major communities were established in upper American Fork. One was Deer Creek, located near where Tibble Fork Reservoir is today. The other was Forest City at the base of Mary Ellen Gulch.

Work began in the early 1870's on a narrow gauge railroad to transport ore from Forest City. A roadbed was dug all the way up the canyon, but construction was terminated in 1872 at Deer Creek, as the route above was too steep and tortuous. At about this time American Fork was struck by an epidemic of diphtheria or scarlet fever that killed numerous children and some adults. Many of the more God-fearing Utahns felt that this was punishment for yielding to the temptations of selfishness and greed, and for degrading the canyons that were so vital to their way of life.

The mines gave out completely in 1876, and in 1878 the railroad closed. The tracks were removed for salvage, so all that remains today as a reminder of this period is a roadbed, many

---

*It didn't turn out quite as planned! "Utah contains a peculiar people," wrote Thomas D. Brown in 1865 while visiting New York in an effort to market Utah mining stocks. "They pay no taxes, charge high for provisions, and are unsafe to dwell amongst."

Brigham Young did not care much for the miners either. "We cannot eat silver and gold," he claimed. "Neither do we want to bring into our peaceful settlements a rough frontier population to violate the morals of our youth, overwhelm us by numbers and drive us again from our hard earned homes."

Figure 8-1—In the early 1960's the U.S. Forest Service spent great amounts of time and money for terracing and revegetation of over-grazed areas. It has been estimated that the restoration process will take about 100 years. Four generations of taxpayers will thus pay for the ignorance and greed of the few.

trails and abandoned mines, and scores of names. There must be fascinating stories behind Graveyard Flat, Mary Ellen Gulch, Major Evans Gulch, Van's Dugway, Miller Hill, etc.

Without the exploratory efforts of one man, George Tyng, the mining era of American Fork Canyon would have come to an end in 1876. In 1901, with his credit almost exhausted and with his "last stick of dynamite", Tyng broke into a new rich vein, thus starting a second mining boom in the area. His discovery led to a fifty year prolongation of this activity †, a period that

---

† Probably the most tragic consequence of the two eras of mining activity in American Fork Canyon, as indeed throughout the western U.S., was the permanent transfer of valuable public lands into the hands of miners and other private interests. Much of the takeover of local canyons by developers can be traced back to the antiquated "Mining Law of 1872", which legalized the giveaway. One notable reversal of this process occurred in 1937, when Mayor Watson deeded 700 acres of land in the Alta area to the federal government for public winter recreation.

195

saw five aerial tramways constructed for hauling ore down from various mines. One of them went all the way from Tibble Fork to upper Mary Ellen Gulch, and operated until 1951.

During the early 1900's, the overgrazing branch of the local free enterprise system also took advantage of profit possibilities in American Fork Canyon. Thousands of sheep could be found in the Wasatch Mountains at that time. Grazing was of such intensity that slopes did not have time to revegetate during the short growing seasons of this arid alpine area. The cloudbursts that come in spring and fall still pose a flood threat to the valleys below. Fig. 8-1 is another reminder of the importance of long-range planning.

Even today's "environmentally conscious" generation threatens American Fork Canyon. A paved highway "to make the canyon more accessible" has been promoted to replace the old railroad bed which has been smoothed by a generation of horses and recreational vehicles. Development of two new ski resorts has been proposed for upper American Fork Canyon, and Snowbird has expressed an interest in expanding operations to the summit of American Fork Twin Peaks and an additional 8,000 to 10,000 acres. (Responsible tourers and other outdoorsmen must be constantly aware of pressures exerted by commercial interests in the canyons. They should actively participate in the planning processes to prevent further exploitation of their public lands.)

Ski touring routes in American Fork are generally longer and the snow less predictable than for most of the tours described in preceding chapters. Many of the runs are on south-facing slopes, so avalanche conditions usually stabilize rather quickly, but the snow also softens and can become mushy and hard to ski during warmer periods of the day. In late afternoon these slopes are often icy and even more difficult to navigate.

Perhaps the least attractive aspect of American Fork Canyon tours is the necessity for long car shuttles. A drive from Salt Lake City to Tibble Fork is about 30 miles. The additional 20 mile drive to Alta means that approximately 100 automobile miles may be driven, a disconcerting distance for energy-conscious tourers*.

Rather than dividing up the chapter into intermediate and

---

*While energy consumption is a concern of most tourers and hikers, it seems to be of little consequence to ski area developers. The Utah Travel Council spends great sums of taxpayers' money to attract out-of-state skiers regardless of how much petroleum is used to get them here. Worry about the "Energy Crisis" was certainly short-lived.

advanced tours, we have included sections on three geographical areas. The first is upper American Fork Canyon, which contains the majority of the tours. Second is the South Fork of American Fork, which contains the Alpine Scenic Loop and the northeast slopes of Mount Timpanogos. The chapter (and book!) are concluded with a description of two tours in Dry Creek, a small canyon sandwiched between American Fork and Little Cottonwood.

UPPER AMERICAN FORK CANYON

The most notable feature of tours into upper American Fork is their extraordinary length, which is at least ten miles. Because of this and the unpredictable snow conditions on the southern slopes, these tours can be either delightful or exceptionally challenging and dangerous. Thus, it is impractical to classify them according to difficulty. The first three tours (see Fig. 8-2) are somewhat easier than others in this area, but even these often require more than intermediate skills.

There are two common starting points for skiing into upper American Fork. One is Alta, and the other is White Pine Canyon in Little Cottonwood. Tours from Alta are quite straightforward. Each succeeding route described is more difficult and dangerous than the one before. Some require an ascent of American Fork Twin Peaks, the highest point in the Little Cottonwood ridge. They all conclude with a descent of one of the gulches to the main canyon below. (See numbers (1) through (7) on the map.) Ski tours starting at White Pine are the most difficult of any in American Fork Canyon. Routes (8) and (9) cross from upper White Pine and Red Pine, respectively.

Dry Fork

Dry Fork is the eastern branch of upper American Fork Canyon. It terminates near Sunset Peak just above Lake Catherine in Big Cottonwood Canyon. A good starting point for a run down Dry Fork is the Albion hut at the head of Albion Basin. The ascent route from Alta is described in Chapter 7. It is basically a climb to the top of the Albion ski lift, a traverse up to Catherine Pass, and a ridge run to the hut. This involves a 1700 foot elevation gain over 2.7 miles.

From Albion hut one traverses gently downward and to

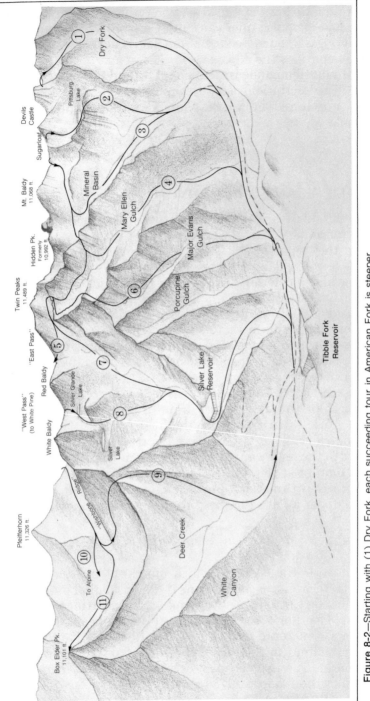

Figure 8-2—Starting with (1) Dry Fork, each succeeding tour in American Fork is steeper and more difficult than the one before. (2) Pittsburg Lake, (3) Mineral Basin, and (4) Mary Ellen Gulch involve considerable traversing, but have very little elevation gain. (5) White Pine Canyon, (6) Major Evans Gulch, and (7) Silver Creek require an ascent of the summit of Twin Peaks. Route (8) into Silver Creek starts in White Pine, and routes (9) Deer Creek, (10) Dry Creek, and (11) Box Elder Peak are best initiated in Red Pine.

the right (directly south) for about 0.4 mile where a series of relatively steep, but under safe avalanche conditions very skiable, slopes lead into the bottom of Dry Fork Canyon. This drainage can be followed all the way to the main American Fork Canyon. It is also possible to traverse along the right side onto the lower section of the ridge separating Dry Fork from the main canyon. This alternative provides some relief from the monotony of the long, relatively flat trek to Tibble Fork.

The junction with the main canyon is 3.5 miles and 2,800 feet below Albion hut. Either of two very prominent jeep trails can be followed for the next 1.3 miles until they merge and follow the old railroad grade to the reservoir. Total descent is 8.7 miles and 4,100 feet. The last seven miles are most enjoyable on touring skis, so this tour is best done when the snow at the higher elevations is suitable for this type of equipment.

Pittsburg Lake

Pittsburg Lake is a small glacial tarn nestled beneath the summit of Sugarloaf. It is accessible from near the top of the Sugarloaf lift at Alta. The lake was named after the old Pittsburg Mine, which contained only low grade ores, but nevertheless remained active until 1924. Two wooden tramways, operated by gravity, once carried ores from this mine into American Fork Canyon below.

The Pittsburg Lake tour starts at Alta and ascends the Albion and Sugarloaf ski areas to Germania Pass between Mount Baldy and Sugarloaf. When climbing up the downhill ski trails, be sure to stay well to the side to avoid impalement by the flailing masses of humanity going in the opposite direction. A short hike from the pass takes you to the summit of Sugarloaf which overlooks much of Little Cottonwood and American Fork Canyons. This climb is 2200 feet over 2.4 miles.

From the peak, you can ski along the crest of a ridge that goes directly south. From this ridge a steep couloir leads down into the upper, treeless section of the cirque just beneath the peak. Stay to the right in order to avoid a band of cliffs and follow the drainage down through relatively open slopes to the lake. From there the route flattens and then follows an old mining trail to the canyon bottom. Nearly the entire ski tour route is visible in Fig. 8-3. This photo can also be used to pick more challenging and interesting descent possibilities from the summit of Sugarloaf.

The main jeep trail leading down American Fork is usually

Figure 8-3—The summit of Sugar-loaf overlooks Pittsburg Lake which lies in a glacial cirque south of the peak.

on the right side of the canyon, just a few hundred feet above the stream. The descent from Sugarloaf to Tibble Fork Reservoir is 8.8 miles, 4,600 feet.

Mineral Basin

One of the most popular touring routes in American Fork is the descent from Alta into Mineral Basin, which is a large cirque at the head of the main canyon. The crest of this impressive cirque is defined by American Fork Twin Peaks, Hidden Peak, Mount Baldy, and Sugarloaf.

Mineral Basin gets its name from the many mines once located there. One in particular owned by Jesse Knight, deserves our special attention. It was located below some fairly large avalanche paths. Nearby miners were being killed by snowslides right and left, but Jesse wanted no part of that. Ingeniously, he built his boarding house, an impressive two story building made of 10 inch timbers, into the slope of the hillside, with a roof that allowed the snowslides to pass right over the building. His boarding house was so well designed that much of it still remains today, although partially collapsed due to excessive weight on the roof from lack of snow removal during the past 50 years.

The easiest way into Mineral Basin is via Alta's Germania Pass, or Snowbird's "Gorilla Pass".* Germania is located between Sugarloaf and Mount Baldy and is the safest alternative. Gorilla is located between Mount Baldy and Hidden Peak.

Three common descent routes into Mineral Basin are shown in Fig. 8-4. Routes A and B are totally downhill from Germania Pass. The first stays on the steep east side of the upper bowl, and the other follows more moderate terrain down the center. Once inside the basin, simply follow the main drainage, staying to the right so the jeep road leading out of the canyon can be intercepted. The climb to Germania Pass is 2.2 miles with 1700 vertical feet to gain. The run down to Tibble Fork is 9.9 miles and 4,100 feet.

MILLER HILL. A side tour from Mineral Basin that involves very little additional climbing is Miller Hill, between Mineral and Mary Ellen Gulch. This 10,264 foot summit was named after Jacob and William Miller of Park City, who had a claim on the hill in the late 1860's. In 1871 they sold their interests to the New York City Aspinwall Steamship Co. for $120,000. The steamship firm developed Miller Hill into the leading ore producer in American Fork Canyon. After yielding more than $2 million worth of gold, silver, copper and lead, the mine gave out in 1875. Shortly thereafter it was leased by George Tyng who continued to work the mine. After many fruitless years, Tyng finally struck it rich in 1901 by discovering a new vein. He became a wealthy and respected man, but was killed

---

*Knowledgeable tourers will recall that "Gorilla Pass" was named in honor of Snowbird

executives who promoted their resort by showing a giant ape trampling the summits of upper Little Cottonwood Canyon. A portion of their billboard is shown at left. The ape has become a symbol of the destruction of our canyons by developers. (Photo courtesy of Citizens Committee to Save Our Canyons.)

Figure 8-4—Mineral Basin, surrounded by five 11,000 foot peaks, is the upper end of the main branch of American Fork Canyon. Most ski tours into the canyon start at one of the high passes in this basin. Routes A and B go directly down the drainage. Routes C and D are traverses into Mary Ellen Gulch.

by an avalanche. Tyng was buried near the top of Miller Hill, where his gravesite can be found today.

Route C in Fig. 8-4 shows the approach to Miller Hill from Germania Pass. A higher traverse can be taken, but the avalanche danger increases very rapidly at greater elevations. It is possible to descend directly from the hill into American Fork

Canyon or into Mary Ellen Gulch. Since many routes are possible for either alternative, no specific ones have been marked on the photo. The reader can use the illustration to choose a descent that is within his abilities.

Mary Ellen Gulch

Mary Ellen Gulch is another popular ski tour in American Fork Canyon. After considerable research at several libraries, the identity of Mary Ellen is still a mystery to the authors. Was she a madam or a missionary? Perhaps she was one of the local "girls" for whom so many western mining camps have been named. One unconfirmed story claims Mary Ellen to have been a cook at a miners' boardinghouse, who became lost and perished under bizarre circumstances in a nearby tunnel complex.

Mining activity in and around Mary Ellen Gulch was of such magnitude that a town was built at the bottom in the early 1870's. Forest City was described as a "progressive city with a profitable saloon and a lady school teacher from Salt Lake City". The Sultana Smelter, 15 charcoal kilns, and a kiln for the preparation of lime operated nearby.

Mary Ellen Gulch rises about three miles from Dutchman Flat in American Fork Canyon to a large cirque beneath Twin Peaks. Figure 8-5 shows the entire gulch and can be used to locate a number of mining roads for descent. The 'standard' route into Mary Ellen Gulch follows route C of Fig. 8-4 to the pass just north of Miller Hill. This was described in the Mineral Basin section. From this pass (also visible in Fig. 8-5) the descent is fairly routine, basically following the left side of the drainage until it joins the jeep trail at the junction with the main canyon. This tour requires a 1700 foot, 2.2 mile climb to Germania Pass, with a total descent of 8.5 miles and 4100 vertical feet.

American Fork Twin Peaks

For those who like to ski Mary Ellen from a higher elevation and especially for those who wish to ascend the 11,489 foot summit of American Fork Twin Peaks, it is possible to traverse higher in Mineral Basin and to intercept the Mineral Basin-Mary Ellen Gulch ridge at the 10,400 foot level rather than the 9,800 foot pass near Miller Hill. This is considerably more hazardous than the routes described in the Mineral Basin section, but it does save about 600 feet of climbing.

The tour starts at Alta or Snowbird and crosses into Mineral Basin from Germania or Gorilla Pass. It then follows

Figure 8-5—Mary Ellen Gulch was one of the most active mining areas in the Wasatch Mountains in the 1870's and again in the early twentieth century. Many remnants of this era remain for today's visitor to observe. Route C drops into the canyon from Miller Hill. Route D continues up to the summit of Twin Peaks.

the long traverse (labeled D in Figs. 8-4 and 8-5) beneath Hidden Peak and into upper Mary Ellen Gulch. Ascent of the steep headwall beneath the Twin Peaks summit is an especially dangerous undertaking. Don't attempt it unless you are 100% certain of safe avalanche conditions. Fig. 8-6 shows the Mary Ellen cirque and the expansive summit block of American Fork

Figure 8-6—American Fork Twin Peaks is the highest summit in the Little Cottonwood-American Fork ridge. It actually has four peaks and is part of the drainage of six major side canyons (all coveted by ski area developers). Routes shown in the photo are (D) to White Pine, (E) Major Evans Gulch, (F) and (G) to Silver Creek.

Twin Peaks. The climb from the Alta parking lot is 2700 vertical feet over 4.6 miles.

Alta to White Pine Canyon

Until the advent of helicopter skiing and the accompanying rise in noise pollution, the tour from Alta to White Pine Canyon was a favorite of many Utah tourers. Some feel that despite the presence of this nuisance, it is worth doing at least once each year. Although the route is relatively simple, it is extremely hazardous, requiring caution along its entire distance.

The tour starts at Alta or Snowbird and goes over either Germania or Gorilla Pass. The route is an extension of the ascent of American Fork Twin Peaks, so it follows route D in Figs. 8-4, 8-5, and 8-6. From the summit of the Twins, take a long, gently-downward traverse to the right around the large basin that lies between the four peaks. This leads to "East Pass" of White Pine Canyon, which is shown in Fig. 8-7. This traverse is not at all trivial, for it crosses one of the largest, steepest, and most feared avalanche slopes in the Wasatch.

The Upper White Pine section in Chapter 7 (Fig. 7-6) can be used to choose a route into White Pine Canyon. Distance from Alta via Germania Pass is 5.4 miles, with a total climb of 2700 vertical feet. Descent from East Pass to the Little Cotton-wood highway is 3.5 miles, 3100 feet.

Major Evans Gulch

Major Evans Gulch is the next side canyon below Mary Ellen. It was named after a railroad engineer who "could build a railroad anywhere if he had enough money". Unfortunately for him, the grade excavated for the proposed railroad to Forest City was too steep, and additional money from his employers was not forthcoming. The railroad was stopped at Deer Creek.†

The tour from Alta follows route D in Figs. 8-4, 8-5, and 8-6 to the summit of American Fork Twin Peaks, a climb of 2700 feet over 4.6 miles. Only the upper sections of Major Evans (route E, Fig. 8-6) provide good skiing. The remainder of the gulch is a narrow, winding ravine that joins the main canyon just above "Zee-dugway," the only switchback in the American Fork Canyon jeep trail. The entire gulch is pictured in Fig. 8-8,

---

†Unfortunately for us—and for the next generation of taxpayers—the Utah legislature may furnish public funds to finish the project that free enterprise failed to complete. It would not, however, be a railroad, but a paved highway up American Fork Canyon. This has been a "pet project" of some local Utah Valley politicians.

208

Figure 8-8—Major Evans Gulch is a narrow winding canyon that terminates just above the switchbacks in the American Fork Canyon jeep road. Route E descends into this drainage from the summit of the Twins. Porcupine Gulch, in the left side of the photo, is a densely wooded gully that is not suitable for skiing.

showing many mining roads that can be used to avoid the brush and trees in the bottom of the gully. The descent from American Fork Twins summit to the junction with the main canyon is 4500 feet over 3.8 miles. From the junction to Tibble Fork Reservoir is another 2.6 miles with 600 feet of elevation loss.

PORCUPINE GULCH. Porcupine Gulch is an area skied only by those hapless tourers who wander into it by mistake, or by those few tourers who genuinely love dense forests (either aspen

209

or fir!) and steep, narrow, and brush-covered ravines. If your appetite is whetted by such an invitation, see Fig. 8-8 for consultation prior to attempting the tour.

Silver Creek

Silver Creek is a seven mile long canyon which has two branches. The eastern branch descends directly south from the summit of American Fork Twin Peaks toward Tibble Fork Reservoir. The western branch contains Silver and Silver Glance lakes, and terminates with the summits of Red and White Baldy peaks along the Little Cottonwood divide.

Three routes are described for descent into upper Silver Creek. The first two start at Twin Peaks and are labeled F and G in Figs. 8-8 and 8-9. The third route enters American Fork Canyon from "West Pass" of White Pine Canyon. This is number 8 on the map (Fig. 8-2).

SILVER CREEK FROM TWIN PEAKS. The most practical alternative for a Silver Creek tour is to start at Alta or Snowbird and climb to the summit of the Twins as described in a previous section. You can then ski directly into Silver Creek via the large bowl between the peaks (route F). Note in Fig. 8-9 that this involves descent of a series of steep open slopes that are interspersed with cliff outcroppings. Great care is needed in this area.

The second route from the summit is a variation which requires skiing down the south ridge of the Twins toward Major Evans Gulch. Instead of entering the Gulch, however, you can veer directly south and descend a steep, avalanche-prone bowl into Silver Creek. This route is labeled G in Fig. 8-9. Also visible in this photograph are numerous avalanche paths which should be carefully avoided.

At the bottom of the steep upper slopes, the Silver Creek drainage levels off and the vegetation gets thicker. The route crosses Silver Lake Flat, which is a summer home area near the Silver Lake Reservoir. A jeep road goes over into the Deer Creek drainage and down to Tibble Fork. This is a much better alternative than staying in Silver Creek, which has heavy brush and usually marginal snow conditions at that elevation.

The descent from Twin Peaks is 7.2 miles and 5100 feet.

SILVER CREEK FROM WHITE PINE CANYON. A more demanding and challenging route into Silver Creek requires ascent of White Pine Canyon to the 10,700 foot "West Pass" just above

Figure 8-9—The Silver Creek drainage houses two lakes and a reservoir. Routes F and G drop into this drainage from Twin Peaks. East Pass of White Pine Canyon is in the upper left corner of the photo.

White Pine Lake on the Little Cottonwood-American Fork Canyon divide (Fig. 7-6). Descent from this pass into Silver Creek is extremely difficult and hazardous. There are some cliff bands just beneath the pass that require removal of skis or some exceptionally competent skiing.

At the base of the steep upper slopes of the western branch of Silver Creek is Silver Glance Lake, and another half mile below that is Silver Lake. The terrain in this area is quite moderate, but the open, south-facing slopes are exposed to much sun and wind action. Thus, the skiing is usually not as good as in the narrower gulches described earlier in this chapter.

The route from Silver Lake Flat to Tibble Fork is the jeep road mentioned previously. The climb to West Pass from Little Cottonwood highway is 3100 feet over 3.7 miles. Descent into American Fork Canyon is 4300 feet over 6.3 miles.

Deer Creek

Deer Creek is the most westerly tour that is practical in upper American Fork Canyon. In fact, the south-facing exposures and low elevation at the bottom can render it quite impractical much of the time. But the scenery is superb with outstanding views of Box Elder Peak, Mount Timpanogos, and the Utah Valley. This tour should only be attempted by experienced skiers who are familiar with the terrain and competent at route finding.

A tour into Deer Creek starts with an ascent of Red Pine in Little Cottonwood Canyon, as described in Chapter 7. From Red Pine Lake, climb to the ridge that separates Little Cottonwood and the Dry Creek drainage. A good route in upper Red Pine Canyon is shown in Fig. 7-9. Total climb from the bottom of White Pine is 3000 feet over 4.4 miles.

From Red Pine ridge, pick a good spot to drop down into Dry Creek. Now you can enjoy about 1000 vertical feet of downhill skiing before climbing to the pass at the head of Deer Creek. Stay as far left as possible when descending upper Dry Creek, and cross the ridge to the south when it becomes less steep and rocky. This ridge is the north branch of the "Wishbone" shown in Fig. 8-2 and described in the Dry Creek section later in this chapter. An upward traverse to the south branch of the Wishbone gets you to a point overlooking Deer Creek and the Tibble Fork Reservoir at its lower end.

A jeep road goes part way up the bottom of the Deer Creek drainage, but there is less brush and better skiing terrain on the east side of the canyon. The descent from the Red Pine ridge to Tibble Fork is 6.2 miles with a 4200 foot vertical drop.

SOUTH FORK OF AMERICAN FORK CANYON

There are many ski touring possibilities in the South Fork of American Fork Canyon, but only six are described here. The first two are much simpler than the others. One is the Alpine Scenic Highway, and the other is the road to Sagebrush Flat.

212

Figure 8-10—Six tours are described from the Alpine Scenic Highway, which goes between Provo Canyon and the South Fork of American Fork Canyon. They are (1) the Alpine Scenic Highway, (2) Sagebrush Flat, (3) the north peak of Timpanogos, (4) Timpanogos Basin, (5) Roberts Horn, and (6) Mount Timpanogos from Aspen Grove.

213

The last four tours all involve an ascent of extremely steep and hazardous terrain on spectacular Mount Timpanogos. All six tours are shown in Fig. 8-10, a composite photo and map.

Alpine Scenic Highway

The Alpine Scenic Highway, labeled 1 in Fig. 8-10, is a popular route both for men and snow machines. The gradient is gentle, and there is almost no avalanche danger over the entire eight mile length of the highway that is left unplowed in winter. The distance to the Scenic Highway summit is only about four miles and less than 1500 vertical feet from either Aspen Grove in Provo Canyon or Mutual Dell in American Fork. The tour can be started in either canyon and cross to the other. If a car shuttle is unavailable, one can return to the starting place. A third alternative is to split up into two groups with one starting from each side; just don't forget to switch car keys in the middle.

Sagebrush Flat

About two miles up from Mutual Dell along the Scenic Highway is a spur road leading to the right. A few hundred yards up the spur is the Timpooneke Guard Station and associated picnic areas and campgrounds. Further beyond that, another road continues to the right. This roadway (route 2 in Fig. 8-10) proceeds in a winding, gently-upward climb for about five miles to the north end of Sagebrush Flat, a large meadow between the north peak of Timpanogos and Mount Mahogany. It is obvious from the photo that this road passes under areas of immense avalanche activity, so the tourer is urged to choose another outing in uncertain snow conditions.

From Sagebrush Flat the panorama of Utah Valley, Utah Lake, and Utah's steelmaking centers is outstanding. It is second only to the same scene viewed from the summit of Mount Timpanogos itself. The climb from Mutual Dell to the north end of Sagebrush Flat is 2000 vertical feet. Descent can be either back along the roadway to Mutual Dell, or south across Sagebrush Flat and down to the town of Pleasant Grove.

Mount Timpanogos

At 11,750 feet, Mount Timpanogos is one of the largest and most scenic mountain massifs in Utah. Its long crest forms a

Figure 8-11—The usual view of Mount Timpanogos from the west is this spectacular sight. The peak is nearly eight miles long, most of which is more than 11,000 feet above sea level. It is one of the highest peaks in the Wasatch Mountains.

spectacular backdrop to a number of Utah Valley communities. During periods of intensive atmospheric inversions in Utah Valley, this is the only peak protruding through otherwise impenetrable layers of haze and smog. Figs. 8-10 and 8-11 show two views of the spectacular profile that prompted the Indians to give it a name which means "Sleeping Maiden".

Because of its immense size and a relatively good management policy by the Uinta National Forest (who have designated it a "Scenic Area"), Mount Timpanogos is basically intact despite the pressures of "modern" man.

This is a delightful area for enjoyment of winter solitude. Even beginning tourers can find spectacular vistas from the lower parts of the mountain. Unfortunately the high elevations have the most avalanche activity of any mountain in Utah. All of the tours described in this section are highly alpine in nature and should be attempted *only by knowledgeable and experienced ski tourers and mountaineers.* Snow conditions are particularly critical. Very few people attempt a Timpanogos tour until very

215

Figure 8-12—The north peak of Mount Timpanogos looms menacingly above the jeep road to Sagebrush Flat. This is not a safe place to be unless snow conditions are absolutely stable.

late winter or early spring when conditions are very stable.

Tour descriptions in this section are intentionally brief. Anyone venturing into the area on skis should be intimately familiar with the terrain.

NORTH PEAK OF TIMPANOGOS. The 11,383 foot north peak of Mount Timpanogos can be climbed from the north end of

216

Sagebrush Flat by ascending straight up the steep west ridge leading to the summit. This requires some rock scrambling, but most of the severe avalanche slopes can be avoided. The route is shown in Fig. 8-12. (Note also the steepness and size of slopes above the Sagebrush Flat Road!)

The distance from Mutual Dell to the summit is nine miles with 4800 feet of elevation gain. The last 2800 feet of climb is done in less than two miles!

TIMPANOGOS BASIN. During late spring when avalanche conditions have stablized, a growing number of Utah Valley tourers ascend into Timpanogos Basin via the Timpooneke hiking trail. The photographic insert in Fig. 8-10 shows the complexity of the terrain below the Basin, with numerous large rockbands (named appropriately the Giant Staircase). The climb from Mutual Dell to the Basin is 4000 vertical feet.

From Timpanogos Basin one can ascend another 1200 feet to summit of Timpanogos, or climb over the saddle to the south toward Emerald Lake and the rest cabin located there. Descent from the Basin can be either back down the "staircase" or by traversing to the south around Roberts Horn and skiing down into Aspen Grove via Primrose Cirque.

THE CLEAVER. Ascent of The Cleaver* is one of the more fascinating tours in the Mount Timpanogos vicinity. Although the scenery along this route is unsurpassed, it is not a tour that is often attempted. The best time to climb The Cleaver is in late spring or early summer after the Scenic Highway has been plowed and opened to vehicular traffic. This allows you to start from the summit of the highway, so the ascent to Roberts Horn is only 2900 feet. This summit is shown in Fig. 8-13. It is obvious from the photo that one must be careful where he steps on this "tour."

From Roberts Horn one can continue to the summit of Timpanogos via Emerald Lake, or descend into Timpanogos Basin and ski down the Timpooneke trail. Another option is to descend into Aspen Grove via Primrose Cirque.

MOUNT TIMPANOGOS FROM ASPEN GROVE. Aspen Grove is a small community of summer homes near the south end of the Scenic Highway. It is located 1.6 miles north of the Sundance ski resort owned by celebrated actor and prominent environ-

---

*"Cleaver" is a term commonly applied to prominent ridges or summits which split, or divert, glaciers. At one time this area was glaciated and this ridge split the Timpanogos glacier into separate drainages. Although its summit is officially known as Roberts Horn, the entire ridge will be referred to in this text as "The Cleaver".

Figure 8-13—Roberts Horn at the upper end of the Cleaver is a challenging winter climb.

mental spokesman, Robert Redford. A popular ski tour from this area is the climb to the summit of Mount Timpanogos via Primrose Cirque (labeled 6 in Fig. 8-10). Primrose Cirque is a steep canyon bordered on one side by The Cleaver and on the other by Elk Point. Both peaks send avalanches onto the trail below, so this tour should not be attempted under any but the safest avalanche conditions.

The route from Aspen Grove follows almost entirely the Mount Timpanogos hiking trail, so familiarity with the area in summer is important. For the initial 0.8 miles from Aspen Grove, the trail goes along the bottom of the drainage, which is relatively flat. For the next mile, however, it zig-zags mercilessly as it ascends 2600 feet to the hanging valley that contains

Emerald Lake. The summit is another 1700 feet above the lake.

DRY CREEK CANYON

This book would be incomplete without a description of the touring possibilities in Dry Creek, a small canyon located between American Fork and Little Cottonwood. Dry Creek starts near the community of Alpine and ascends to the northeast until it terminates at the pass between the Pfeifferhorn and White Baldy. The 11,101 foot Box Elder Peak is along the south flank of Dry Creek.

Several routes that have been mentioned previously (the ascent of the Pfeifferhorn, the tour into Bells Canyon, and the descent into Deer Creek) skirt along the upper portions of Dry Creek Canyon. The Red Pine to Alpine tour described below descends the entire length of the canyon. A good understanding of its topography is also helpful for anyone climbing Box Elder Peak. Unfortunately, the slopes that must be skied on these routes face mostly to the south and west, and snow conditions are often marginal. Like American Fork Canyon, superb scenery makes up for much of your suffering.

Red Pine to Alpine

Even though this tour requires a lengthy car shuttle, it has remained a very popular route since the late 1920's. The tour starts at White Pine trailhead in Little Cottonwood Canyon, and follows the route described in Chapter 7 to the ridge above Red Pine Lake. (See Figs. 7-6 and 7-9.) The climb is 4.4 miles with 3000 feet of elevation gain.

From this pass the *theory* of the descent to Alpine is straightforward; just follow the drainage to the town of Alpine. The *reality* is not that simple! The canyon is wide, and it is possible to miss the route and become trapped in several miles of thick oak brush near the bottom. The secret of success is to find the jeep road that goes the entire length of Dry Creek, before the vegetation gets too dense for skiing.

Fig. 8-14 shows the upper part of the canyon. The first mile of descent is in an open bowl. Many tourers like to angle to the south in this area and stay on the northwest slopes of Wishbone Ridge. Others prefer to traverse high, just below the summit of the Pfeifferhorn, and ski the south-facing slopes below the peak into the bottom of the Dry Creek drainage. The jeep trail is on the south side of the canyon, and can usually be found

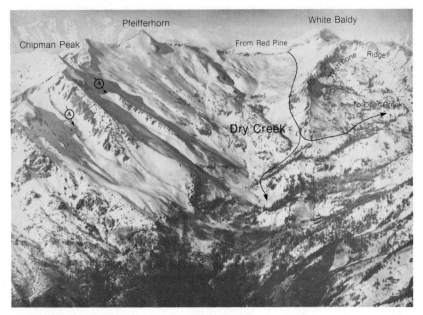

Figure 8-14—Dry Creek is a small canyon between Little Cottonwood and American Fork Canyons. It enters Utah Valley near the town of Alpine.

with little difficulty.† The run down to Alpine is 5.7 miles and 4900 vertical feet.

Box Elder Peak

Box Elder Peak is one of the areas that was severly damaged by overgrazing during the first half of the twentieth century. It was also the site of a bad cloudburst in the 1950's which sent a wall of water rushing down Phelps Canyon near the bottom of Dry Creek. The Dry Creek Powerplant at the mouth of the canyon was destroyed, and rocks the size of a pickup truck were deposited where none were before. As a result of years of uncontrolled grazing—*and only one rainstorm*—the upper slopes of Box Elder were serrated with erosion gullies thirty feet deep.

Tourers who reach the summit ridge of Box Elder Peak will be impressed not only with the spectacular vistas of Mount Timpanogos, Utah Valley, and the Little Cottonwood divide, but also with the immense efforts exerted by U.S. Forest Service

---

† If you have trouble finding the jeep road, just listen for the snowmobiles. This is a popular area for them, and skiing the lower section of the road often resembles a roller coaster ride!

Figure 8-15—The north cirque of Box Elder Peak is an impressive sight at any time of year. The east ridge of the cirque is a relatively safe climbing route.

personnel in contour trenching this area to stop further erosion and flooding. (See Fig. 8-1.) The trenching is usually visible even in winter and will probably be there for centuries to come.

There are three common routes to and from Box Elder Peak, all starting in different canyons: Deer Creek in American Fork Canyon, Red Pine in Little Cottonwood Canyon, and Dry Creek. The climb can be done as a one or two canyon tour. Whichever alternative is chosen, it is necessary to get to the ridge shown in Fig. 8-15 between Dry Creek and Deer Creek. The final 1800 foot push to the summit is along this ridge. The ascent is 4.8 miles and 4700 feet from Deer Creek, 8.4 miles and 4700 feet from Red Pine, 5.3 miles and 5400 feet from Dry Creek. Descent routes are the same. □

Notes:

Notes: